Preparing for Christian Marriage

Preparing for Christian Marriage

Marriage

Pastor's Manual

Antoinette & Leon Smith

ABINGDON • NASHVILLE

Originally published as Pastor's Manual for
GROWING LOVE IN CHRISTIAN MARRIAGE
Copyright © 1981 by The United Methodist Publishing House

Abingdon Edition *Preparing for Christian Marriage*
published 1982

Library of Congress Cataloging in Publication Data

SMITH, LEON, 1918-
Preparing for Christian marriage.
Bibliography: p.
1. Marriage.   2.   Marriage counseling.
I. Smith, Antoinette.   II. Title.
BV835.S58   248.4   80-28001   AACR2

ISBN 0-687-33918-9
ISBN 0-687-15930-X (United Methodist ed.)

Manufactured by the Parthenon Press at
Nashville, Tennessee, United States of America

To Bette and Don,
Jim and Marcia,
and Mark and Pat and Andy,

from whom we are learning
much about growing in love.

Foreword

This Pastor's Manual is designed to be used with PREPARING FOR CHRISTIAN MARRIAGE, the couple's guidebook on preparing for marriage. It was prepared by a team of highly qualified persons—the authors working closely with an editorial committee of five other couples and a panel of thirty-eight consultants who reviewed the manuscripts.

Designed for use with the couple's guidebook, this manual suggests ways you can help couples prepare for Christian marriage, both in groups and in premarital counseling sessions. We believe you will find it useful to have each couple fill out the "Premarital Questionnaires" in the back of their guidebook and discuss their answers in the context of their premarital sessions with you.

You are urged to have on hand copies of the couple's manual, PREPARING FOR CHRISTIAN MARRIAGE, to present to each couple you marry. We hope your church will provide these.

We are grateful to the authors, the editorial committee, and the consultants for their careful work in preparing these manuals.

We trust that these manuals, prepared with the hearty cooperation of so many competent people, will prove a blessing to thousands of couples as you and other pastors guide them in PREPARING FOR CHRISTIAN MARRIAGE.

Contents

Chapter 1
Preparing for Marriage Is Important

The phone rings. It is Phil Gordon sharing the news that he and Peggy Jones are engaged! You share his excitement. They want you, their pastor, to perform the ceremony. They know you expect to see them as soon as possible. So you set the date for their first session.

As you hang up the phone you sit there for a moment. You feel a sense of joy that this couple want to make adequate preparation for their marriage. You ask yourself, "How can I do my best for them?"

We believe you care about Peggy and Phil—and all the couples you marry—and are concerned about improving your skills in helping them prepare for marriage.

We see you as a busy pastor with many other urgent matters demanding your attention. Quite likely you turned to this manual because you expect it to give you some help with this important part of your work. In a very personal way we will share with you out of our forty years of ministry and marriage.

We assume that you know your church expects you "to perform the marriage ceremony after due counsel with the parties involved." You want these sessions to be more than simply planning the details of the rehearsal and the wedding. You also want them to be more than reading over the ritual and discussing it with the couple, important as that is. We believe we can and must educate persons for marriage. This workbook, used with *Preparing for Christian Marriage* (hereafter referred to as the couple's workbook), is written to assist you with a variety of ways for helping couples prepare for marriage.

According to a study by G. K. Hill on ministers in The United Methodist Church, nine out of ten of those pastors (actually, 94 percent) insist on meeting with engaged couples for purposes other than the rehearsal one or more times before they will marry them. (This 94 percent is made up of 73 percent who always insist on premarital sessions and 21 percent who usually do.)[1]

It may be that you are one of those who received some training in pastoral counseling in seminary, but perhaps only two or three hours of the entire course were devoted to preparing for marriage. Only a little more than half of you (53 percent) have had any training in this field, either while you were in school, or in workshops or seminars since leaving school. Training, for the majority, has been limited to only a few days at pastors' school or in a workshop.

When Hill checked on the take-home benefits of such training, he found that less than one out of five pastors rated this training as "highly helpful," while 29 percent said it was only "moderately helpful." Perhaps this is why more than half of you expressed a desire for additional training in premarital preparation.

Some seminaries are now offering more training in premarital preparation and counseling, especially in short courses at summer school or as part of a regular semester course in case studies.

You Want Help Now

In your case, however, you may feel that you cannot wait several months or a year for such training. You want help now. You want to do some reading and studying on your own. Of course, a book cannot substitute for more adequate training through formal courses, pastoral training in an accredited setting, or clinical supervision by a well-trained counselor. But we believe this book can give you some guidelines in the direction of more adequate preparation for marriage.

But why are you concerned about premarital preparation now? Does your concern grow out of an immediate situation with a couple you are now seeing? If so, you may be tempted to turn to the section of this manual that deals with that particular subject. But remember, such an approach is likely to lead you to look for specific techniques or easy answers, rather than basic understanding. Actually, understanding *who you are*, the context in which you work, and what it is you are trying to do, are far more important than methods. Such understanding must grow out of your *being yourself*, a minister of the gospel, in relationship to people. This manual attempts to give you some help in each of these areas. It is a resource for finding the methods that will best express your style of ministry.

Your motivation for improvement may also arise out of some unhappy past experience. Maybe you feel bad about the last couple you married. Perhaps they had a special problem that needed attention. You knew about it, but they did not bring it up. You were not sure how to raise the subject. And now you are worrying about not giving them as much help as you think you should have given.

Or your feelings may go even deeper. Perhaps one of the couples you married recently is already getting a divorce. Now you are questioning your ability. We hope you can keep such anxiety from driving you to despair and can direct it into constructive channels for improvement. We do not underrate the positive value of anxiety, of course, but we hope you will remember that you are not expected to be perfect or always to get perfect results.

Many pastors have a strong drive to succeed. This may cause some to try to do too much for a couple. This manual is intended to assist you in doing your best to help a couple and leaving the rest in their hands. Remember, you are not responsible for others. Of course you care *about* them, but we think that that is quite different from taking care *of* them. When you have done your best, you can commit the situation to God and leave it there.

You Care About Families

Your desire to improve your skill in premarital preparation may grow primarily out of your concern for people's welfare. In your various contacts with the families in your parish you may have discovered a great deal of marital unhappiness.

Some pastors estimate that from 25 to 40 percent of the persons in their congregations each Sunday are unhappy in their marriages. Although these pastoral estimates may seem high, they are not as high as those made by professional marriage counselors, who state that half the persons married today are unhappy. This is not to say that all of them are contemplating divorce. But it does indicate that a large percentage of couples are struggling with severe difficulties with which they need help.

Even though no authentic research is yet available to support our hopes, many of us believe that premarital preparation can be an effective preventative of trouble. Not that it is a cure-all. We know better! But we do believe that it has real value. Many couples indicate that it does, and a number of authorities agree.[2]

The High Divorce Rate

The extremely high incidence of divorce may be another reason for your concern about your training and practice in marriage preparation. And rightly so, for the United States has the highest divorce rate of any country in the world. Of course we do not know if premarital counseling, as presently practiced, is effective in preventing divorce. But we do believe pastors can increase their effectiveness, and that is the purpose of this manual.

In some large cities the high divorce rate is appalling. In some metropolitan counties, as many divorces are granted as marriage licenses issued in a given year. Some people think these figures mean that half of the marriages are ending in divorce each year. However, many couples granted a divorce in the urban county were actually married one, two, or three years earlier in another county, perhaps in a small town or rural area.

A more accurate comparison is the ratio of divorces in any given year to the total number of marriages in our population. This ratio includes couples who married two, ten, twenty, or fifty years ago (all of whom are potential divorcing couples) and is not limited to those who marry in any one year. On this basis, there was roughly one divorce for each fifty existing marriages. Such a figure compares the actual number of divorces in any one year with all the marriages that might possibly end in divorce at that time. At the present time approximately two-thirds of all married couples live together "until death us do part."

Many authorities used to think that children were a deterrent to divorce and cited statistics to indicate that the majority of couples getting divorces did not have children. But that was before 1957. Since then, the majority of divorcing couples have had one or more children. And divorce seems to be much more difficult for children than for adults.

A few years ago pastors sometimes recommended that couples contemplating divorce have a baby to solve their problem. Not so any more. Now many pastors realize that for a couple in conflict to have a child only adds to their problems and diminishes their resources. It also exposes a child to possible serious damage.

You might say "divorce runs in the family." One study found that the divorce rate was much higher among couples whose parents were divorced. In marriages where the husband and the wife came from homes where there had been no divorce, the divorce rate was only 14.6 percent. But if the parents of one of the partners had been divorced, the couple's divorce rate probability increased to 23.7 percent. If the parents of both partners had been divorced, their divorce rate probability climbed to 38 percent.[3] Of course this study does not mean that children whose parents are divorced can never have a happy marriage. But it does alert us to the fact that they may need some conscientious assistance in making intelligent preparation for marriage.

While we are on the subject of divorce, perhaps we should add that *teen-age marriages are especially likely to end in divorce*. For example, a person who marries before age seventeen is three times as likely to get a divorce as one who marries at age twenty-one. Another way to say the same thing is that approximately one-half of all teen-age marriages end in divorce. In addition, the best estimates are that in one-half of all teen-age marriages the bride is pregnant before marriage.

A sobering thing about teen-age marriage is that nine out of ten of these weddings are performed by pastors in their home churches. This raises the question: How much premarital preparation are pastors doing and how helpful is it?

Maybe each time you see one of these marriages breaking up, or each time you try in vain to help a couple in conflict find their way to reconciliation and to a satisfying life together, you promise yourself that you are going to do a better job with the next couple you marry.

Most of you, we believe, want to do a better job of helping couples prepare for marriage because *you care about what happens to persons*.

One of the most important functions of the Christian church is to help people live fulfilled lives. As a pastor you represent the church and can help a couple lay a good foundation for achieving fulfilled lives through their marriage. Apparently Jesus intended that people experience fulfillment when he said, "I came that they may have life, and have it abundantly" (John 10:10b). No doubt you believe that the abundant life is for all persons, and for most, that life includes marriage. Indeed, we believe you see marriage as one of God's good gifts which, when accepted and used rightly, dignifies and enhances life.

You know, however, that for many persons, marriage is a disappointing and degrading relationship. This stimulates you to try to find better ways of enabling couples to experience a mutually satisfying life together. Premarital preparation can make an important contribution to the enhancement of marriage from the very beginning.

Marriage Is Important

Preparation for marriage is important because *marriage* is important—both to the persons involved and to society in general.

In the first place, marriage is important because of *the number of persons* involved. Approximately 95 out of 100 persons in this country marry at some time during their lives. It is estimated that nine out of ten first marriages are performed by clergy. Obviously this presents you with a real challenge—an opportunity to minister to a large number of persons at one of the most critical periods in their lives.

Second, *marriage is important to the persons being married*. Marriage is an intimate, living relationship in which a man and a woman may help each other to meet their needs. This includes their need for companionship and ego-support as well as their sexual needs. Marriage is an opportunity for personal fulfillment and self-realization for both partners.

Marriage does not necessarily guarantee a satisfying sexual relationship, but it does provide the socially approved framework within which couples may find their way to sexual fulfillment.

In our society today there are so many depersonalizing influences that make us feel like numbers or cogs in machines instead of human beings. Is it any wonder then, that husbands and wives are expecting more of each other than ever before, especially in the area of their personal affectional needs? Many men and women are aware of the fact that they do not really know who they are as persons until they "find themselves" in an intimate relationship such as marriage. After experiencing this self-realization, these persons describe their former selfhood as incomplete.

Many of us have other close interpersonal relationships to help meet our fellowship needs; as we should have, of course. But to cope with our basic sense of loneliness, most of us need deeper companionship, and we believe a satisfying marriage can provide this. There is a real sense, then, in which we can become whole persons as our lives are complemented by our mates and as many of our needs are fulfilled by our life together.

Another social factor making the quality of marriage more important to the married couple today is mobility. When young couples move away from their parents, they are more dependent on each other.

In addition to the quality of the relationship, *marriage is also important because of the length of time a man and a woman are a married couple,* as opposed to being children or to being parents. Most people in the United States today live together as husband and wife, without children in the home, longer than they were children in the parental home, or longer than they are parents with their own children at home.

The average woman today is married shortly after her twenty-second birthday. (Her husband is usually about two years older.) She usually has her first child by the time she is twenty-four (from eighteen months to two years after marriage) and her last when she is twenty-six or twenty-seven. Since most children leave home at eighteen, this means that her last child is launched when she is forty-four or forty-five. With a life expectancy of about seventy for her husband, she has about twenty-four years of marriage left. Although she is a wife as well as a mother during the years the children are at home, we might sum up by saying that she spends twenty-two years as a "child," twenty years as a mother (and wife), and twenty-five years as a wife without children at home.[4]

Since our culture puts so much emphasis on parenthood and parent-child relationships, it sometimes comes as a surprise that the average couple spend more of their married life without children at home than they do with children at home.

Marriage is important to children, both in their development as persons and in their preparation for marriage.

Today marriage is the foundation of the family and provides the atmosphere, or climate, in which children are born and reared. For healthy development as a person, a child needs the security and warmth of a stable, loving relationship between the mother and father. Family therapy is revealing that children with emotional problems are often victims of troubled marriages.

For example, a person who does not find his or her companionship needs met by the marriage partner may turn too much attention to a child. The child's life may be warped in the process. On the other hand, family therapy is also showing us that parent-child conflicts may contribute to marriage problems.

Positively stated, the best preparation for marriage we can give our children is a sound marriage of our own. The best preparation is not some formal instruction on how to succeed in marriage. Rather, it is the experience of living in the context of a satisfying marriage—a marriage in which the partners are able both to cope with problems and tensions (that are inevitable in close human relationships) and to enjoy the pleasures and rewards these relationships make possible. In such a climate children can learn to be themselves, and are free to be open and trusting. They can learn the fundamental and essential skills of communication, as well as the process of decision-making and problem-solving on the basis of mutually established goals and values.

Stressing the critical value of marriage to children does not mean that parents shoulder total responsibility for all the influences on children. Families live in the midst of many forces affecting their lives.

Marriage is important to society, for marriage itself is a social institution performing certain functions for the general welfare. Since a family consists of a group of two or more persons related by marriage, birth, or adoption, a married couple constitutes a family. Beyond this, however, marriage is the foundation of the family with children. The family is a basic unit of society. We believe it is the primary unit.

What are some of the services provided by the family as a social institution? Marriage, as we have seen, is the socially approved framework in which men and women may join in meeting their needs as sexual beings. Further, marriage is still the most socially approved relationship for child-bearing. The family is responsible for bearing enough children to keep the world populated (but not overpopulated!). The family is also an institution essential for child-rearing, meeting the child's needs for physical, emotional, social, and spiritual growth, particularly in the early years.

The family is a context for transmitting the culture and conserving the fundamental values on which the culture is based. But the family not only conserves and transmits values, it also makes possible change and improvement from one generation to another.

With its provision for privacy and security for its members, the family serves as the matrix for the formation of attitudes and values, thereby shaping the very structure of our society.

Even though some social scientists believe that the family is facing a period of declining influence over members of society, as compared to the influence of political and economic institutions, many others are pointing out the important values that families are contributing to society. For example, when family members are willing to sacrifice for one another and are loyal to one another because they believe loyalty is grounded in reality, to this extent society is infused with a sense of the dignity and worth of persons—a basic value. Likewise, when family loyalty and the sacredness of the marriage commitment are honored, family relationships are strengthened, and society, in turn, gains some of its basic social motivation. Dependable, functioning marriages contribute enduring qualities to the very fabric of society.

Both as a structure of society and as a channel of God's love, *marriage is important to the kingdom of God.* In the wedding ceremony we say that marriage "is an honorable estate, instituted of God." This means that we believe marriage is a form of human relationship given by God in creation. We believe that God ordained marriage. However, deciding whether or not to marry is an individual matter, and we affirm the right of each person to discover God's will for him- or herself. Pastors have an opportunity to "help people become free to choose marriage or singlehood."[5] But what we are writing about here is marriage, and we want to emphasize that marriage is one of God's good gifts, which may be accepted, used, and enjoyed.

Marriage may also become the channel for God's love. God is the source of love. Even though God has an unlimited number of ways of coming into this world, one of the most effective ways is through the love of a man and a woman for each other. The marriage relationship may convey God's unconditional love; a love that sacrifices, forgives, sustains, affirms. When this love is shared, not only between husband and wife, but also with their children and, beyond the immediate family, with others in the community and world, to this extent is the kingdom of God a reality.

As we stated above, premarital preparation is not a cure-all. Nevertheless, helping couples prepare for marriage is vitally important. Marriage preparation has special significance for the pastor who feels a keen sense of responsibility because of the opportunity it gives for ministering to persons. This is especially true when we realize that this ministry is performed in the context of the Christian faith and community—to which context we turn in the next chapter.

The fact that you do your premarital preparation within the context of pastoral ministry adds some significant dimensions to your work. After all, you are a pastor—a minister of the gospel—and not a psychiatrist or family physician. The unique dimensions of the pastoral context will be considered here in these topics: (1) What it means to be a pastoral counselor/educator; (2) expectations of the pastor; (3) the Christian faith and community; and (4) the pastor and the couple.

What It Means to Be a Pastoral Counselor

What does it mean to you to be a pastor or minister of the gospel? How does this affect premarital preparation? This is asking the basic question, Who are you? And the equally important question, What difference does your *being* make in this aspect of your ministry?[1]

A pastor is one who *cares* for people. This care is not only a genuine concern for all that happens to people as whole persons in all their relationships (with themselves, others, the world, history, and God), but a concern that emphasizes the dimension of the spiritual and eternal in all these relationships. In fact, we believe that the overarching goal of all pastoral care is fostering the spiritual growth of persons, both in relating to God and in relating to one another.

This caring is expressed in action, in the shepherding functions of healing, sustaining, guiding, and reconciling. In premarital preparation these functions provide different ways of bringing the whole gospel through the person and ministry of a pastor to an individual or couple(s) contemplating marriage. The particular form of preparation for marriage may involve you with an individual, a couple, or a group, although most often we think of the couple relationship.

Healing centers on helping individuals to overcome the hurt and brokenness in their lives and to become whole persons. It is obvious that very little can be done in this area in the rather limited number of sessions usually allotted to preparation for marriage, but this basic concern for health and wholeness will always be present. On occasion, you may be sought out several months before the wedding and given an opportunity of sharing in the growth of a person toward wholeness, which we see as so essential for a "healthy" marriage.

For example, a widow may be approaching a new marriage, but still have a grief problem to work through. Or a divorcée may have been hurt so severely in a previous marriage that healing takes months. Such persons may require depth counseling over a long period of time, which might mean the postponement of remarriage.

The pastoral-care function of *sustaining* has to do mainly with supporting or strengthening a person to cope with a situation or condition that cannot be changed. This may mean helping a person to accept and adjust to a handicap or limitation, his or her own or the partner's. Or it may take the form of supporting one or both persons through a brief period of uncertainty—if that is all it is. Much so-called premarital panic is a form of anxiety arising from fears that have been buried. This panic may signal the need for professional help to enable such a person to deal with the fears. In any case, it is important not to reassure the person too hastily or superficially. For if there is a real fear underlying the uncertainty, this needs to be dealt with directly and not be covered up.

Perhaps most people think of preparation for marriage primarily as *guiding,* that is, as being mainly instructional or educative counseling, with the pastor taking the initiative and doing most of the talking. This may happen in groups, with a couple, or with an individual. Actually, educative counseling does include the giving of information, but we think it is much more than this. It is helping persons make decisions and plan for the future in the most constructive manner possible under the circumstances.

In this kind of educating you help a couple draw on their own resources and make decisions for themselves, rather than doing most of the talking yourself. You try to help them to be realistic about the many adjustments they may wish to make in the light of ultimate concerns of the Christian understanding of the meaning of marriage. The couple's manual, chapter 10, will be an invaluable tool here. (See also chap. 3 on a theology of marriage and chap. 9 on educative counseling.)

The *reconciling* function of pastoral care involves the pastor in helping a person or couple face their conflicts and reestablish their broken relationship with each other or with God. This need, for example, may be the result of premarital sexual experiences or pregnancy. It is important not to gloss over difficulties for the couple, but to face them realistically and with understanding love. Such problems usually call for forgiveness and discipline from one or both partners.

A minister of the gospel, then, is a servant who is committed to helping people to know the good news and to live by it. The gospel is the good news of God to persons that adds the eternal dimension to all of life. Thus, as a minister, you share the redeeming love of God with those who have sinned and separated themselves from one another or from God.

As a minister of the gospel you also endeavor to uphold certain values and principles that you believe represent God's purposes expressed in marriage. We hope this does not mean that you will be rigid and dogmatic, but that you have made certain commitments and recognize certain responsibilities. It is important always to remember who you are and what your function is.

Specifically, when you are confronted with a decision about whether to marry a particular couple, you are a minister of the gospel and not a justice of the peace. We believe that performing the ceremony for two persons who see marriage as no more than a temporal legal contract is a violation of your integrity as a minister. On the other hand, it seems to us that it would also be a violation of your integrity if you failed to make available to such a couple all the resources of the gospel and the church at this time of critical need in their lives.

Likewise, because of your integrity as a minister,

you limit yourself to your role as a pastor. For instance, when the need for extensive psychotherapy is indicated, you respond as a pastoral counselor to the limit of your ability. But beyond that limit, you refer the person to a competent professional therapist. You do not attempt to go beyond your limits.

We would emphasize also *your unique training and resources as a pastor*, as contrasted with other counselors. Other counselors may be trained primarily in dealing with the inner dynamics of a person's life or in the field of interpersonal relationships. But your training is usually heavily concentrated in the area of the search for meaning and value, most likely through the study of Scripture, doctrine, or church history.

The absence of training in the field of interpersonal relationships has been one of the major weaknesses of ministerial education, but fortunately this is improving. For clergy deal with interpersonal relationships in all aspects of their work, especially in marriage and family ministries. Even when your training includes personality development and interpersonal relationships, these are set within the larger framework of moral and spiritual values. Your training should equip you to help persons find the meaning of existence, both personal and transcendent. This kind of training, for example, may enable you to help persons appreciate the value of the marital relationship, rather than see marriage as an end in itself.

To be sure, other Christian counselors may also use the resources of the Christian faith—Scripture, prayer, sacraments, devotional literature. But, because of your office, you have a special opportunity to use these resources, whenever appropriate, in your helping. We say "whenever appropriate" because they should not be used as a crutch, or a club, or as a substitute for the hard work of struggling with a problem and searching for a solution in real life.

For instance, a couple may reveal to you that their reason for planning to marry is premarital pregnancy. You cannot immediately turn the couple and the problem over to God in prayer and forget all about the hard work required to find the best possible solution. Instead, supported by prayer and all the other resources of the church and the Christian faith, you have the opportunity to guide the couple in exploring every possible alternative and to help them follow through with the one that seems best for all concerned.

Helping persons prepare for marriage is only one of many

responsibilities you carry as the pastor of a congregation. This is also true if you are one of that very small, but growing, group of ministers today who are giving full time to pastoral counseling as a part of the staff of a large church or in a pastoral counseling center. At times, responsibilities may come into conflict with one another and create problems for you. How do you cope with such conflicts?

When your function as a church administrator clashes with your role as a counselor, what do you do? Take an example: As an administrator you must help make a decision regarding a young woman's continuing to serve as leader of an informal group in the youth fellowship. She is one of your most attractive and dedicated workers. You already know that she had delayed marriage until her late twenties because of the illness and financial need of her mother, now deceased. But in your premarital counseling you learn that she has been having an affair with her employer, and that she is wondering if she should tell her fiancé about it. She is troubled about what this might mean to him. You are concerned about her and about whether she should continue to work with the young people of the church. What will you do?

Or, when your preaching responsibilities threaten to undermine a counseling relationship, what do you do? It is Friday afternoon, and you already have your Sunday morning sermon prepared. In fact, the subject is already printed in the bulletin. You have worked hard to get it all done so you and your family can get out of town just as soon as the children are out of school, and that is only an hour from now. So as soon as you complete this appointment, you are leaving for an overnight stay on the lake with friends. You plan to stay as long as you can and return late Saturday night.

Your appointment is with a young man. You do not know him too well, for only the young woman he plans to marry is a member of your church. But you feel you are beginning to develop a relationship with him. This is the first session with him alone since the two of them filled out their Premarital Questionnaires. You have reviewed the questionnaires and discovered that a major cause of disagreement is their differing views as to whether the church should be involved in social issues. The young woman is very liberal, but the young man is conservative on this point. As the session comes to a close you suddenly realize that you have spent most of the hour (and he has spent most of his emotional energy) on this one area of conflict, and that this is exactly what you are planning to preach about on Sunday!

You know the couple plans to be present. You wonder if they will think you are preaching "at them," or if you are taking sides against one of them in their conflict. It is too late to change your sermon. Or should you, even if you had time? What would you do?

One problem most of you face is finding time to do all that is expected of a pastor. With so many other responsibilities demanding attention, you may find it hard to schedule the premarital sessions. This may be especially difficult when couples work and can see you only in the evenings or on weekends.

Occasionally pastors are criticized by church officials for giving too much time to counseling. It is possible to spend so much time on one part of your ministry that you do not have enough time left for other, equally important tasks. Some pastors spend so much time counseling that they neglect sermon preparation or church administration responsibilities.

It may be especially difficult to find enough time for premarital preparation if several couples are to be married at about the same time. This does happen on occasion. When it does, why not take advantage of the opportunity for group preparation? This approach is often more effective than seeing a couple alone—at least it is an effective way of using some of the counseling time (see chap. 4 on group preparation).

How many weddings do you have in a year? The nationwide study already referred to found that more than a third of the ministers (35 percent) marry fewer than six couples a year. Almost a third (31 percent) have from six to ten weddings a year. This means that about two-thirds of the ministers average less than one wedding a month. If we add to this the 17 percent who marry from eleven to fifteen couples each year, this averages about one wedding a month for 83 percent of the ministers. Less than 13 percent of the pastors in the Methodist church, for example, have sixteen or more weddings a year.[2]

As an overall average, three-fourths of the ministers who serve a church of less than nine hundred members have about one wedding a month. Usually when pastors have more than one wedding a month they are part of a multiple staff serving a larger congregation. In addition to group work, if you should average four or five one-hour appointments with each couple you marry, most of you would be giving a little more than an hour a week to premarital preparation. Some couples, of course, will require more time than "the average."

Expectations of the Pastor

Because you are a pastor, *couples have certain expectations with which they approach you*. Some of these expectations are positive, and others are negative, when related to preparing for marriage. They may be based, not on personal contact or direct experience, but on a generalized conception of what couples think a pastor is supposed to be or do.

Most people expect help from their pastor. In fact, they may turn to you more often than to anyone else. Perhaps you are aware of the nationwide study done some time ago that found that one out of seven adults had sought professional help with a personal problem.[3] Forty-two percent of them went to their pastors, 29 percent to their family doctor, 18 percent to a psychiatrist or psychologist, and 10 percent to an agency such as Family Services. Of the Protestants who attend church at least weekly, the figure was even higher—54 percent went to their minister.

You may feel that it is different with preparation for marriage. You may be finding it difficult to get some couples to come to you in time to schedule as many interviews as may be necessary for working in depth. Perhaps their expectations have something to do with their readiness to come.

Most people probably see you as a religious authority figure. They may look up to you with a warm feeling of trust and confidence. These feelings may lead some persons to come to you with a sense of dependence, looking for "answers" or some "good advice." They may want to shift to you their responsibility for decision-making and may expect you to tell them what to do. Others may react against the image of authority, strongly resisting any kind of help from you.

Because the minister is regarded as a protector of the morals of the community, you may be expected to be judgmental, condemning those who make mistakes. On the one hand, a person who feels "in the right" may talk very freely about a partner's wrong-doings, expecting you to take sides. On the other hand, a person may hesitate to "confess his or her sins" for fear of being condemned. Because of this nearly universal expectation, you may be the last person in the community to learn about a particular problem, such as a premarital pregnancy. And many people may be very reluctant to talk with you about their sex feelings or experiences.

You need to be aware of these feelings and to discover their meaning to the persons so that you can deal with them creatively, both for the growth of the persons involved and for the improvement of their relationships. Otherwise you may be at sea, wondering what is going on and failing to give the constructive help that is so desperately needed.

Most of you are known to your congregation as married men or married women, though some of you are single. Parishioners probably know your spouse and have some feelings about the quality of your marriage. Your people may be encouraged to come to you for premarital preparation when they know you are happily married. Most persons, however, find it hard to accept the fact that pastors have problems, either in their personal lives or in marriage, and knowledge of such problems may deter some. The pressure on the pastor to demonstrate a happy marriage may cause some pastors to cover up problems and to refuse to seek help when it is needed.

If you have encountered some marital problem, you may be more sensitive to the needs of others, but you may be more vulnerable too. We know you do not have to be perfect or free from all problems to be a good pastoral counselor. But we believe you have to understand yourself, your needs, and your problems enough so that your problems do not control you and cause you to seek substitute satisfaction through your helping relationships. Generally you are able to be a better pastor when you are a healthy, wholesome, mature person and are having your own needs met outside the helping relationship.

For us this means accepting one's humanness and the partner's, too! Our experience with clergy and spouses is that those who discover that conflict is a natural part of a growing depth relationship become more real persons. Learning to use conflict creatively so that both partners are valued and respected brings the couple closer. And what a relief to get down off the pedestal!

For the married pastor, we suggest that you ask your spouse to take about an hour to share in the following experience. Separately, each of you should list (1) Three things I like about our marriage, (2) Three things I'd like changed in our marriage, and (3) Three things I'm willing to do to improve our marriage.

Be as specific as possible. When both of you have finished your lists, share them with each other. As you listen, try to understand the other's feelings without being defensive or judgmental. Try to accept feelings as they are, not counting them right or wrong. When each of you has felt heard and understood (not necessarily agreed with), take turns responding to each other. The important difference, as we see it, is in *responding* rather than *reacting*. Finally, each of you is asked to decide on your first "next step" as a way of implementing your decisions.

If you are a single pastor who has never married, you probably often feel pressured to be married. (The pastor who was previously married and is now single may also feel these pressures.) We want to affirm you in your state and acknowledge your freedom to make your own decisions. We hope you will claim your own strengths and contributions in facilitating growth for those preparing for marriage.

As a single person you have your own unique experience with marriage; beginning with the marriage of your parents and the marriages of friends and parishioners you know well. We believe you can be helpful to couples preparing for marriage when you reflect upon these experiences and incorporate their meanings into your own value system and then share with the couples you work with.

Here is an experiment we would like to ask you to do. Plan to take about an hour. List the ways your parents showed their love and concern for each other. From this list identify the values you have gained for yourself and brought into your ministry.

Then list the things you missed or wished for from your parents' relationship. What effect has each of these had on you and your ministry? Do the same for married friends and parishioners you have observed at close range.

Take time to reflect on your feelings and which values you deliberately choose to cultivate in your own life. What is the first step you could take to foster these values? You may want to discuss and clarify these feelings with a trusted friend.

Closely related to their expectations of the pastor are *the feelings engaged persons have about the place in which the premarital sessions are held.* The actual physical setting has some meaning for most persons, and this meaning may facilitate or impede growth.

Most ministers do their premarital counseling in the church building, usually in the pastor's study. Group sessions usually are held in a classroom. Some of you may be forced to use a corner of the sanctuary. A classroom with a door that can be closed is usually better than the sanctuary, especially for counseling. In smaller churches sessions may be held in the parsonage. Any of these locations still symbolizes "the church" to most people.

What is significant here is the fact that the church building symbolizes something to each individual. For most persons, the church represents God. A person who believes God is loving and forgiving is likely to respond positively to meeting with you in the church. Another person, who conceives of God

as a tyrannical judge bent on punishing offenders against divine law, is likely to react negatively—at least initially, or until firsthand experience with you as a warm, caring person changes his or her mind. Is it not wise, then, to be sensitive to what the church symbolizes to particular people?

The Christian Faith and Community

To do premarital preparation in the pastoral context means that you are undergirded by the Christian faith and work as a part of the Christian community. You operate not in a vacuum, but within a definite frame of reference. For example, you counsel not as a lone professional but as a member of a group—the pastor of a congregation.

The Christian faith focuses on the double dimension of the divine and the human, the vertical and the horizontal relationships. These include not only a person's relationship to God as revealed in Jesus Christ, but also a person's relationship to others. This double dimension provides some guides for the formulation of basic positions on faith and morality. We are concerned here especially with the implications of the Christian faith for persons in the marriage relationship. (An expanded explanation of these implications is given in chap. 3.)

Each pastor must think through his or her own position regarding such important concerns as the Christian understanding of marriage as a covenant relationship. We think it is important for you to be aware of your basic assumptions and just how these affect your marriage preparation. We hope that you will not want to impose your views on others, but that you will be aware of your basic beliefs and why you hold them. When you are sure of your position, we believe you can permit others the freedom to find their own way.

You already have some understanding of the nature of persons. Out of this understanding arises your style of working with people, your way of relating to others. True, you may not have thought this out very carefully. Perhaps you cannot explain it to others with clarity. But you have some base from which you work, and we think awareness of this base allows you to work consistently and with some sense of direction. With this awareness we believe you will be able to modify your basic assumptions when experience dictates that it is necessary.

In the area of morals, for example, you operate one way if you believe that morality consists of a set of laws that have been given by God at some time in the past and are passed on, unchanged, to each new generation. On the other hand, you operate in an entirely different way if you believe that every individual is responsible before God for his or her own actions and must discover God's will for him- or herself in each particular set of circumstances. What is your own position, and how do you see it influencing your group work or counseling?

Closely associated with the Christian faith is *the Christian community that receives, sustains, and transmits that faith*. The Christian community is the setting for both the pastor and the couple. It is from this setting that you work. In most instances it is also the setting in which the couple belong. In your marriage preparation you see the man or the woman not as an isolated individual but as a member of a community—a church. Many times, of course, it may be only the woman who is actually a member of your congregation. Her fiancé may be from another community. If he is, usually he is welcomed by the congregation and treated as if he actually belonged.

The church is a special kind of community, whose goal is to be one that cares what happens to persons and to their marriages, one that shares in the significant moments in their lives, in times of crises or in high moments of celebration and rejoicing. It is a community that shares, to some extent at least, a common set of values, and experiences a sense of fellowship and common purpose.

Today the church recognizes the importance of the ministry of the laity. We believe that *you as a pastor have invaluable resources within the congregation for helping persons prepare for marriage* (see chap. 4 on group preparation). As spiritual guide, you have the opportunity to call your members to be a caring community, to help your church, as Charles Stewart describes, to be "the family of families."[4]

The church certainly may help persons prepare for marriage through the ongoing program-curriculum, either in week-by-week teaching/learning experiences, or through certain events. These may include discussion groups in the youth fellowship or in church school classes, and leaders may make use of a variety of resources, such as books and films. Groups may consider such subjects as understanding oneself, the meaning of sexuality, the ethics of sex, dating and courtship, and the meaning of marriage. Such an informal group or personal growth group for young people is an important aid to personal maturation that will be helpful in all relationships, including marriage. In addition, the church may provide more formal courses or weekend retreats on preparation for marriage, or group marriage preparation for engaged couples (see chap. 4). And, of course, there is premarital counseling!

The church also places a great deal of importance on the wedding ceremony as a high moment of celebrating a marriage. The church sees the wedding as a service of worship in which two persons take their vows before God in the presence of the congregation. This emphasizes the religious significance of the event as the formal initiation of the couple into a new state of life—"in holy matrimony." The wedding also focuses attention on the sacredness of marriage as a covenant relationship (see the couple's workbook, chap. 10).

The Christian community may help to sustain a couple in their life together by *providing continuing enrichment of their marriage across the years*. The church recognizes the two persons as a married couple in a variety of ways. For example, a special group may be provided for them, such as a church school class or couples' club for married persons. These groups afford couples the opportunity to work together to resolve some of the issues and problems with which they are struggling. The church may also provide marital growth groups that focus specifically on enriching and strengthening marriage.[5]

Although very little is said about it today, the Christian community still has a disciplinary function. This is manifested in the expectation that a couple will honor their vows and uphold each other in love. To be sure, this is not discipline in the punitive sense. Rather, it is discipline through nurture and instruction, as the couple find their life together in the congregation, or as they take advantage of helpful resources.[6]

And, if trouble should come, the services of the pastor are available for marriage counseling. In fact, more than half the counseling the average pastor does involves marriage problems. (For many people this fact raises the question of how well the pastor is trained to do marriage counseling.)

The Christian community also helps keep a couple from making an idol of their marriage. The church challenges a couple to look beyond their own immediate needs and satisfactions, to see themselves as "the church" in the community where they live, and to live in the world with a sense of mission in fulfilling God's purposes for them as a married couple.

The Pastor and the Couple

One of the distinguishing qualities of premarital preparation in the church is the relationship of the pastor and the couple. For other professionals the counseling relationship is the sole relationship between a counselor and a couple. For pastors, however, there are actually three stages of relationship—before, during, and after the premarital sessions—each of which is a phase of the continuing pastoral care relationship.

For example, when a woman calls her pastor "to set the date for the wedding," the contact may then open the way for premarital preparation. Sometimes this is her first contact, but the caller probably has known you through the worship services of the church. From your sermons she already has formed some opinion as to the kind of person you are. This may be true of the man as well. Very often, however, because of the custom of having the wedding in the bride's church, the groom may be from another community.

In some cases both the man and the woman may be unknown to you. But this is usually the exception rather than the rule. It happens more often in downtown city churches, in churches in county-seat towns where marriage licenses are issued, or in churches with beautiful sanctuaries or chapels. Nevertheless, the couple have a set of expectations about the relationship, generalized perhaps from previous contacts with other pastors in years past. Most persons have some kind of notion of what pastors are like, and from this they draw their own conclusions about what your helping a couple prepare for marriage will be like, and such conclusions may or may not be accurate.

On the other hand, the contacts between you and the couple may have been rather extensive and in a variety of settings. You may have visited in the home, perhaps on a get-acquainted basis, or, more likely, at a time of crisis in the family. The couple may have known you in a number of groups in the church. Some of these contacts may have been formal, others very informal. In some instances you may have shared in the leadership of a class for youth on preparing for marriage to which the couple has belonged. These earlier contacts, whatever they were, have established some kind of relationship between you and the couple. And these can influence the couple's relationship with you in the premarital sessions, either positively or negatively.

When you have had a prior relationship with a couple, you need to remember that *the nature of the relationship changes when you move into premarital counseling*—whether group, couple, or individual sessions. And you need to help the individual or couple to understand this change in relationship.

This may be difficult for some couples, but it is the pastor's responsibility to differentiate and clarify the nature of the new relationship.

In premarital preparation the nature of the relationship changes because of its purpose, content, process, and structure. *The purpose of the new relationship is to help a couple prepare for marriage.* This is much more direct and specific than most relationships. The goal is to help this particular couple prepare for marriage. This is not preparation for marriage generally, but for *their* marriage. Usually they will marry, not sometime in the distant future, but soon, which may add a sense of immediacy or urgency to the relationship.

The content of the premarital sessions is their lives and relationship, their problems and plans—not research findings from the experiences of others. The focus is on their feelings and attitudes, their values and dreams. Their strengths and weaknesses, their capacities or handicaps are of crucial importance. This means that the pastor-couple relationship is more intimate and personal than most others, for it deals with private and confidential matters not usually shared. At best, there is an openness and honesty about the relationship, a free sharing of problems and concerns. Of course there will be times when individuals or couples are not ready to talk about certain things. Some may be embarrassed or afraid. We think it is important to deal with the embarrassment or fear. You will be providing a climate of trust that will encourage the couple to feel free to express their deep feelings, whether positive or negative.

On the surface, the process of the sessions may appear to be only conversation, much of which is initiated by you. To be sure, you may give some instruction, but most of the time you will be trying to ask the right questions and listening to the feelings and the meanings behind the words. *You will be trying to help the individuals understand themselves and their needs, their relationships and circumstances.* You do this to facilitate their making their own plans or solving their problems themselves.

The relationship between you and the couple in premarital preparation, then, is structured differently from other relationships. For one thing, it is strictly confidential. The couple need to know that the sessions are limited in time and place to the set interviews in your study or other designated place. They need to be assured that every time you see them—whether in the congregation, in a committee meeting, or on the street—you are not going to be reviewing the details of their last session, especially if the session involves problems.

Although you discipline yourself not to take the experience out of the office, it is very difficult for the couple to do the same. They are likely to be self-conscious and sensitive about even unintentional references or situational elements. Thus it may be best to address this subject with the couple. You simply cannot isolate your marriage preparation from all other relationships, nor should you. You will continue to see couples on various occasions.

The important thing, of course, is for you not to worry about any contact outside the designated sessions, but to make clear to the couple that in premarital preparation you have a different kind of relationship.

After the marriage preparation is concluded, the couple is not left entirely alone. *One hopes they will be supported by the Christian community.* In addition, they may have a continuing relationship with you as members of the congregation. But if the sessions are helpful, your pastoral relationship will most likely be on a much deeper level afterward. In any case it is important for you to help the couple shift gears from the relationship that focused on their marriage plans into whatever other relationships are continuing. In other words, it is important for you to bring closure on the premarital preparation, even though the possibility of their coming to see you is always there should the need arise.

At the conclusion of the sessions most couples will know that you care about them and are able to give them help if they should ever need it. This can be very reassuring to most couples.

Some couples, however, may need guidance in how to continue their relationship with you. They may expect to receive tidbits of help whenever they see you. You, on the other hand, need to be sensitive to signals for help and guide the person or couple into counseling. Of course you do not want to make a major case out of every comment, or be too eager to get a couple to come in for counseling. But you do need to gauge the seriousness of need and to know when to suggest an appointment, or when to leave a situation alone.

If a serious moral problem should be revealed in counseling, you may be concerned about your relationship with the person after the counseling is concluded. Experience seems to indicate that the continuing pastoral relationship is weakened or endangered only when the counseling was not helpful, the problem was not resolved, or the guilt was not relieved. On the other hand, even when counseling is not effective in resolving problems, the relationship may not be affected adversely if you were seen as understanding and helpful.

There have been instances when the situation was so very unpleasant, or the necessary revelation of details so painful, that persons did not want to be reminded of it even by seeing the pastor at church each week. Some such sensitive persons may not attend church for a while until the wound heals. Or they may go to another church or actually move their membership. In some cases this last may be the best solution. Your responsibility is to do the very best you can in counseling and not worry about the consequences in terms of attendance or church membership.

It is good to remember, however, that a sudden change in a person's church attendance habits, either by absence or presence, can be a clue to some personal or family need that may call for some form of pastoral care. Although there is no clear research on the subject, the best clinical judgment is that you do not have to worry about your continuing relationship with those persons who are truly helped to work through their problems, regardless of the depth of these problems. Genuine expressions of concern strengthen the continuing pastoral care relationship and keep the couple aware of the availability of this concern for their well-being.

A critical component of the context of premarital preparation is your theology of marriage. We help you explore this in the next chapter.

Since your premarital preparation is done in the context of the Christian faith, it would be good to explore some of your basic theological assumptions regarding marriage. The purpose of this chapter is to help you think through your own position, for premarital preparation is not a set of techniques to be used in isolation from your basic beliefs or from your vocation as a Christian pastor. Preparation for marriage, including premarital counseling, is a form of Christian ministry, set within a framework of the Christian understanding of the nature of God, men and women and, specifically, of marriage. What follows here is an attempt to describe as briefly as possible some of the basic theological assumptions on which this manual is based.[1]

As we share our basic beliefs with you, we urge you to think through and clarify your own.

The Christian Faith

Essentially, the Christian faith, as we see it, is not primarily a statement of beliefs nor an intellectual assent to a body of doctrine. Rather, to us, it is *living* in the faith relationship with God within the context of the Christian community. It is trusting God as an act of one's entire being. It is responding in faith and love to God as revealed in Jesus Christ. It is permitting God's love to find expression in all the relationships of life, including those between husband and wife and their relationships with others.

How do you describe the Christian faith?

Christian Morality

Since marriage requires many decisions regarding right and wrong, we need to consider the nature of Christian morality. The theme of morality is human conduct, but we believe morality begins, not with human beings, but with God. Righteousness has its origin in God and comes to us as God's command. For us this means that Christian morality is an expression of faith growing out of one's relationship with God. It is not a separate study of conduct on the human level, but an integral part of the meaning of the Christian faith and life.

Christian morality, it seems to us, does not consist of a set of rules for living, nor of certain standards of conduct issued once and for all at some time in the past. God's command is always present, specific, and concrete. Thus it cannot be stated as a rigid rule, for this would result in a legalistic code. However, we readily admit that we are limited human creatures, sometimes deliberately sinful, who need ethical principles to guide our conduct. We also need ethical principles to lead us to Christ, so that in Christ we may come to righteousness through faith (Galatians 3:24; Romans 10:4).

Furthermore, if God's command is always present, specific, and concrete, then we see true Christian morality as the will of God for a particular person, living within a unique complex of relationships, in a peculiar set of circumstances, and at a particular time in history. This dynamic relational concept of morality leaves the way open for change, for discovering new truth.

How dynamic and relational is your understanding of Christian morality?

Personal Responsibility and Christian Community

This understanding of morality means to us that each person is responsible for discovering God's will for him- or herself in each particular time and place—in each event—using the best insights available from all sources.

On the other hand, we recognize that we must be

protected from a fanatic individualism that mistakes our own desires for God's will or that equates the two. We are afforded this protection through following the guidelines of Scripture, tradition, experience, and reason.[2] This protection comes partly by a careful weighing of the command of God as it comes to us in Scripture and in the dynamic tradition of the church. It also comes in the continuing revelation of the Holy Spirit through our experiences and through our reasoning about meanings of these experiences. This process is a thoughtful weighing of the Word and the Spirit as the past is applied in the present.

We see further protection afforded by the contemporary Christian community as the context in which this understanding of the will of God is worked out, for the Christian community can serve to correct and can help to guide individuals in their search (the small sharing group is one way of doing this). On the other hand, an imperfect Christian community—made up of sinners as it always is in this world—must not become a coercive structure controlling the individual. For each person must always be left free to respond to the will of God. At the same time, individuals cannot be left "completely free" to disregard Scripture, tradition, experience, and reason, or the insights and welfare of others. Individuals must weigh all of these carefully whenever they consider making a decision. As Christians, we believe that the one God is at work, both within the individual and within the Christian community, to bring a coherence and wholeness to our understanding of the Christian way of life for all. This calls for a continuing close relationship with God for each person, whether pastor or marriage partner.

How do you relate individual responsibility and Christian community?

Faith in God

Fundamental to the Christian faith is our experience and understanding of God. This may be described briefly as the three persons of the Trinity—God as Father, God as Son, and God as Holy Spirit.

In the first we see God as the creator of all that is. Nothing exists apart from God the Creator. To us God is the "ruler and maker of all things," including persons and marriage. All of life is dependent on God. We believe creation is not a closed event, but continues in the present and into the future.

When we say we believe in "God the Son," we mean that God was in Christ, so that Christ was revealing God's nature, God's love, God's will. The self-giving, victorious love of God is seen especially in the life, death, and resurrection of Jesus. We believe God is revealed in many ways, but supremely in Jesus Christ. This is why we call ourselves Christians and seek to realize the Christian quality of life in marriage.

Through the Holy Spirit, we see God continuing to work in the life of the individual and in marriage as well as within the church. It is through the Spirit that God continues to give us the direction and power we need to live in steadfast love and to do God's will in all things. We are not alone. God continues with us in the midst of all the perplexities and problems of life.

Two other observations are in order at this point. One is that God is the God of all life. Hence we make no distinction between sacred and secular, for God is concerned about every aspect of life, including what we call the most mundane. Nothing is outside God's love and care. The other observation is that we see God as the God of all truth, including the insights from sociology, psychology, education, and other disciplines, as well as theology. Christians, we believe, are under obligation to try to understand and use all such knowledge that is compatible with their understanding of the Christian faith.

How do you express the Trinity and relate it to marriage?

Our Life in This World

At the risk of oversimplifying, we believe there are some fundamental Christian beliefs about human beings and our life in this world that have special significance for marriage. We list them here for quick review.

1. Human beings are creatures of God, created for the kingdom of God, and all of us are of such worth that each person must be treated with dignity and respected as a child of God.

2. God created us female and male, of equal worth. This means that we believe in the equality of men and women as the basis for mutuality in marriage.

3. Although we are limited and controlled by certain "givens" in our background and circumstances, we are essentially free and responsible creatures. We may be obedient to God's will for us, or we may turn away from God in sin, which we often do.

4. We are whole persons who must be understood in terms of all dimensions of our being—body, mind, and spirit. All are interrelated. We cannot be

understood adequately in terms of any one dimension of life alone.

5. In spite of our rebellion against God, we can become aware of our condition, turn, respond to God, and receive the redemption offered in Jesus Christ. By the gift of God's grace we can become "in Christ . . . a new creation" (II Corinthians 5:17; Ephesians 2:8-10).

6. Human beings have certain physical, emotional, and social needs that must be met, but essentially we are creatures in search of meaning. We want to know what is good, true, and beautiful. We have an insistent urge to know the significance of life in terms of ultimate values. To become fully authentic and adequate persons we must find a true sense of personal meaning for ourselves and the whole scheme of things.

7. Life is not fixed. Change is possible even though it is often difficult and sometimes seemingly impossible. In spite of past history and present conditions, God works in the lives of individuals and families to restore broken relationships and bring them to wholeness of life.

8. Human beings are dependent creatures who cannot exist apart from God. Our very existence depends on God's providential care. We can know ourselves truly only in relationship to God. We can overcome the profound evils of life and realize the abundant life only through the grace of God.

9. We are social beings who cannot live in isolation from other people. Our life depends on intimate relationships with a few persons. Our full development as persons will be arrested without wholesome relationships with other people.

10. Although the total demands of the kingdom cannot be fulfilled on earth, the kingdom of God may be realized in this world, at least to an extent far beyond what we now know. Christians are under obligation to acknowledge and demonstrate the reign of God in all areas of life in society.

11. Our life is not limited to this present world. Because we believe in the triumph of life over death, we live for ultimate values and abide in the Christian hope.

You might find it helpful to go back over the above beliefs to identify ways they affect your understanding of marriage. What other basic Christian beliefs would you add?

Marriage Understood Theologically

Against the above background, then, marriage can be understood theologically.

How do you "reason out" the meaning of this human relationship in the light of your understanding of God's nature and purposes for us? We invite you to consider the meaning of marriage in relation to the creative, redemptive, and sanctifying work of God. How do you react to the following statements? What changes would you make?

In terms of *the creative work of God,* we see marriage as one of those structures of society given as a part of creation. This means that marriage is viewed by Christians as a form of human relationship that God ordained for people generally and not alone for Christians. Hence God's intention in the very structure of society applies to all people whether they acknowledge God or not. Marriage, then, is not a convenient pairing of a man and a woman that is contrived by society, but reflects the basic social structure given by God in creation. As we have already pointed out, we do not believe this means that God intends for every person to marry, nor that those who marry are thereby superior to single persons. Rather, we believe this means that God has some particular purposes for marriage, as we indicate below.

God's redemptive activity, we believe, applies to Christians, to those who are redeemed in Christ. In redemption, God forgives our sin and restores us to right relationship both with himself and others; we become "in Christ . . . a new creation." Thus, when Christians come to marriage, they come as new creatures in Christ, seeking to be obedient to God's will for them as individuals and as a couple.

What special qualities do you see Christians bringing to marriage?

In the sanctifying work of God, persons have the possibility of being purified and made holy, with life centered in God. This is an opportunity for husbands and wives to respond to the work of the Holy Spirit as they "grow in grace" and "go on to perfection" by "being made perfect in love." Although we know problems will still plague them, in the process they have the possibility of finding their marriage infinitely blessed.

How do you see the Holy Spirit enabling couples to grow in love—both in loving one another and in sharing their love with others?

As a structure of creation, we understand marriage as having an essential nature and certain purposes that apply to all marriages and not only to marriages of Christians. Christians, nevertheless, may bring certain qualities to the way they fulfill these functions.

How would you state the function of marriage?

*functions
of
marriage*

The four purposes, or functions, of marriage, as we see it, are *union, fellowship, procreation,* and *nurture.* We list them chronologically—in the order in which they usually develop—for we believe it would be a mistake to try to assign a value order to these functions. Each one is of unique importance and is independently valid.

We believe one purpose of marriage is its *unifying,* or *creative,* function. When two people marry they create a new unity without, of course, losing their own individuality in the process. Marriage is, in fact, an intimate relationship in which two individuals of equal worth give up their independence, become interdependent, and find their individuality strengthened and developed by their union. Female and male "become one" in marriage. The partners can aid and stimulate each other's personal growth and development.

Jesus referred to the creation (Genesis 2:24) when he said "The two shall become one" (Matthew 19:5). We interpret this to mean not one physical body or person, but a new dynamic unit—a new functioning, living, growing unity of two persons. The mystery is deep and difficult to understand; nevertheless, it is a fact. This new union may begin tentatively during courtship, but is initiated radically in sexual intercourse. This is one of the main reasons our church urges men and women to reserve sex for marriage. Of course marriage involves much more than sexual union. It is a union of two whole persons, including the physical, mental, and spiritual aspects of their total being.

Another purpose of marriage is *fellowship,* sometimes called the recreative function. God created human beings female and male; persons who are incomplete as isolated individuals. We are made to need communion with one another. In the Genesis account of the creation, "the Lord God said, 'It is not good that man should be alone' " (Genesis 2:18). We believe God instituted marriage as a means of overcoming this aloneness, this incompleteness of individuality, and for meeting the needs of man and woman to complement and fulfill each other.

We do not mean to say that all of one's companionship needs can be met by one person. That would be expecting too much of marriage, would put too much of a burden on one person. We recognize our need for a larger community of persons, of family and friends. Yet marriage emphasizes our need for intimacy and community. At the same time it recreates and nourishes the fellowship between husband and wife, which is perhaps more deep and intimate than in any other relationship.

A significant way of fulfilling the fellowship function of marriage is through sexual relations. Most churches hold that sex is one of God's good gifts. It may be affirmed in marriage by being used to meet the needs for mutual satisfaction of both husband and wife. Sex is not sin, as some people believe, but it may be used for sinful, exploitative purposes either in marriage or outside. Sex is good when it meets the needs of both persons and nourishes companionship, when it helps to strengthen and deepen the sense of fellowship between husband and wife as whole persons.

A third purpose of marriage is *procreation.* It is within marriage, Christians hold, that God intends for life to be conceived and children to be brought into the world. This does not mean that all couples must have children, nor that couples who choose not to have children are somehow inferior to those who do. What it means is that procreation within marriage is the way God plans for continuing the population. With all our concern about population expansion today, however, perhaps we need to emphasize that the admonition to "be fruitful and multiply" does not mean to overpopulate.

Since marriage is a structure of creation, we believe that all people are under obligation to use the vast available knowledge and materials for family planning in keeping with God's will for them. Specifically, our church holds that responsible family planning, practiced in Christian conscience, fulfills the will of God. This means that each couple needs to discover the will of God for them at a particular time and place, taking into account all pertinent considerations such as the physical, emotional, economic, and social factors, as well as their own personal wishes.

A fourth purpose of marriage is sometimes referred to as *nurture,* or the educative or service function. We believe all persons—adults and children—need nurturing throughout life. For adults, marriage is an opportunity for husband and wife to help each other grow to their fullest potential, both as individuals and as a couple.

Since marriage is not intended as an end in itself, one of the purposes of marriage is to so equip and sustain persons that, individually and as a couple, they may be better able to serve others, to make this world a better place in which to live.

Couples who decide to have children are responsible for their protection and nurture. This is the primary, but not exclusive, obligation of parents, since they need the assistance of other persons and agencies. Indeed, it is the responsibility of parents to make the fullest possible use of all appropriate agencies. And it is society's responsibility to see that parents neither neglect their children nor deny them the benefits of society.

Christians emphasize the fact that the educative function of marriage includes the spiritual nurture of adults and children as well as the meeting of the physical, psychological, social, educational, and other needs for full growth.

The Nature of Marriage

As to the nature of marriage, we believe that, normatively, marriage is meant to be *a monogamous, lifelong union based on love and fidelity*, even though many persons do not reach this norm. We find support for this view in our Christian understanding of God's purposes in creation.

For you, what are the essential elements of marriage? What supports do you find for them?

Even though there may be societies in which other forms of marriage are practiced, such as in early Hebrew society when the Old Testament patriarchs were polygamists, we believe that God intends marriage to be *monogamous*. This idea is expressed in our marriage ritual in the words, "forsaking all other keep thee only unto her [or him]. . . ."

In the unifying function, for example, one man and one woman come together to establish a new union, revealed in part through their union in sexual intercourse. This sex act involves the husband and wife in a relationship of "oneness."

Likewise, in the fellowship function of marriage one man and one woman have an opportunity to overcome their isolation as individuals and to meet their needs for female and male companionship, including their affectional and sexual needs. Together they can nourish an intimate relationship in which they "belong" to each other exclusively—so exclusively that the entry of a third party into those areas reserved to marriage, such as sexual intercourse, is regarded as an intrusion and a threat to the union itself.

The value of monogamy is also seen in the procreative function of marriage. Each person is the child of one father and one mother, so that not only one's physical organism, but also one's very existence as a human being is bound up irrevocably with two other persons. All three are bound together indissolubly in the divine structure of creation, not as objects, but as subjects, in a unique relationship as no other three persons ever have been or ever will be bound together.

Similarly, the educative function of marriage requires that husband and wife meet their own continuing needs for mutual support and individual growth. It also requires the cooperative efforts of a father and a mother to give a child the care and protection needed throughout childhood. A child needs a mother and father who are united in a mature and responsible loving relationship.

We also believe that marriage is intended to be *a lifelong union* to be ended only by death of one of the partners. We understand that, in principle, permanence is God's will for all marriages, even though some may fall short of it in practice. The concept of the permanence of marriage is inherent in the very idea of marriage itself, since it is based on the irrevocable nature of the structure of existence given in creation. In reality, a marriage entered into on a temporary basis is no marriage at all. Further, fidelity is a necessary basis for marriage, and must be a permanent quality and not a conditional element in true marriage.

Our United Methodist wedding ritual expresses this principle of permanence both positively and negatively: "so long as you both shall live," and "till death us do part." This does not mean that marriage is to be maintained only as long as it is convenient or pleasing to do so, but for life. In fact, the couple is reminded that difficulties may be expected: "for better, for worse, for richer, for poorer, in sickness and in health."

True marriage, we feel, involves a depth of companionship that cannot grow in an unstable, temporary atmosphere. Deep companionship can be best developed only within a committed relationship. Furthermore, since marriage is the foundation of the family, it needs to be a durable and stable basis for bearing and rearing children.

The fact that some marriages are terminated for grave and sufficient reasons does not change the fact that the intention with which two people enter marriage ought to be to stay together "till death us do part."

If marriage is intended to be a lifelong union, how do you understand divorce?

Divorce and Remarriage

When Jesus was asked about divorce, he definitely stressed that marriage is intended to be permanent, even from creation: "He who made them from the beginning made them male and female . . . and the two shall become one. . . . So they are no longer two but one. What therefore God has joined together, let no man put asunder" (Matthew 19:4-6, see also Mark 10:6-9).

This statement of Jesus we recognize as the ideal, but not necessarily as a binding decree on every person, for we do not believe that he was laying down a legalistic requirement to be applied rigidly in every case. Such a position would be contrary to the general character of his teachings. Further, we believe that Jesus' statement was intended to protect women from exploitation.

To say that a person's choices may contribute to marriage breakdown is not to say that divorce is God's intention; this may be only recognition of a fact in the human situation. Furthermore, insistence on the absolute indissolubility of marriage in every case may be legalistic misuse of a well-intentioned principle. Such legalism fails to recognize the moral right of the exceptional case.

Several other reasons for this view can be cited. One is that we believe God is superior to the creation, God's will is supreme; therefore God is not bound by a structure of society given in creation. We believe further that God wills what is best for the welfare of persons, and what is best for one may not always be best for another.

Another reason for this view is that marriage, like any other social relationship, must be evaluated in terms of what it does to the persons involved—all the persons, including children. Therefore, in particular instances, separation or divorce may be the best possible solution to a marriage that is destroying the persons involved.

More important, however, God's forgiving love as we know it in Jesus Christ leads us to believe that a person is not forever doomed by a mistake, even one involving marriage, but that such a person is capable of entering into a new marriage as a new person.

We believe that remarriage after divorce (or after the death of a spouse, for that matter), should come only after sufficient time has passed for a person to overcome the hurt of the past and prepare for the new marriage. In view of the seriousness with which the Scriptures and our church regard divorce, we think a pastor should solemnize the marriage of a divorced person only when satisfied by careful counseling that (1) the divorced person is sufficiently aware of the factors leading to the failure of the previous marriage, (2) the divorced person is sincerely preparing to make the proposed marriage truly Christian, and (3) sufficient time has elapsed between the divorce and the contemplated marriage for adequate preparation and counseling.

Do you agree with these guidelines? Would you add others?

Love and Fidelity

In our marriage ceremony both the man and the woman promise "to love and to cherish" the partner. One of the fundamental purposes of marriage is to enable couples "to grow in love." This means that we recognize *love* as an essential element in each function of marriage: husband and wife are united in love; their fellowship is deepened in love; they enter into procreation in love; they fulfill their educative function in love. Historically, we may have been late in recognizing love as a basis for marriage; and even today love may be lacking in many relationships. Yet in the New Testament the love of Christ for the church is compared to love in the marriage relationship (Ephesians 5:21-33). We see love, then, as an essential element in Christian marriage.

But we know that love alone is not enough. Love needs to be combined with loyalty or *fidelity* to give a firm foundation for marriage. In fact, fidelity is a necessary element in genuine love; without fidelity there can be no genuine love and no true marriage. But love and fidelity are essential to the performance of each of the functions of marriage—union, fellowship, procreation, and education. Loyalty is seen in the partners' faithfulness to the marriage covenant before God as well as their faithfulness to each other. This involves sexual fidelity, as well as a common loyalty that protects the two from all possible interference from others who might damage any aspect of their marriage fellowship.

Do you see love and fidelity as essential elements in marriage? How do you help couples to appreciate these elements?

Christian Vocation

For the Christian, marriage and family life are understood not only as beginning in the natural creation, but also as coming within the scope of redemption, as finding fulfillment, and continuing in the Christian way of life. When a person becomes a Christian we believe that that person is not freed from these structures of creation, but is empowered to live within them, as, "in Christ, a new creation." Entering marriage as a Christian, we believe, is entering a Christian vocation and a covenant relationship.

How do you see marriage as a vocation?

The concept of Christian vocation has two essential elements: God's call and our response. Our response, of course, may be either acceptance or rejection. A Christian responds in faithful and obedient love.

When vocation is understood broadly, it may be said that there is only one vocation, or calling, for the Christian, and that is discipleship. A Christian is a person who has committed his or her entire life, as a whole person, and all relationships, to God in Christ. In discipleship a person tries to follow Jesus' teaching and example in all the relationships of life—to God, self, others, and the world.

Since God's will is always for a particular person in a particular situation, God calls each person to a specific vocational role in relation to sexuality. Christian tradition recognizes four forms this vocation may take for the Christian. (1) For most persons, that vocation is marriage and parenthood. (2) For some it may be marriage without parenthood. (3) For a few, the sexual vocation may be celibacy—the deliberately chosen lifelong abstinence from marriage and sexual relations for a particular purpose, most often religious service. Protestants insist that celibacy is not a higher calling than marriage or parenthood, but that it may be chosen when the circumstances of a person's whole life are exceptional. (4) Continent witness may be the sexual stance of other single persons than those who choose lifelong celibacy. This stance may be followed for a period of time, such as prior to marriage or after one is widowed, or it may be that a person is celibate for a lifetime—whether singleness is the result of choice or circumstance.

There are also occasionally situations where married partners lead a continent role within marriage for sufficient reasons, such as the extended illness of one or both partners. When persons choose continent witness as a vocation they are not doomed to an empty, fruitless life, but they may find ways to achieve a positive fulfillment as whole persons in the community. Choosing any one of these four sexual roles need not be denial of life, but may be the fulfillment of God's purposes for oneself at that particular time.

Although marriage is ordained for people in general, it is not a command from God applying to all individuals alike. Rather, as we have pointed out, it is a state of life that one may choose. When Christians choose marriage, they do so responsibly, seeking to be faithful to God's will for them in this relationship as in every other area of life.

This means that mature, sensitive Christians do not drift into marriage; rather, they choose it as a deliberate decision of their whole being in response to God's call to marriage as a new state in life. Furthermore, they do not enter marriage with just any person to whom they may be attracted, but with that particular person with whom they sincerely believe they can fulfill God's will. This does not imply that there is only one person in the whole world whom a person should marry. Rather, it means that God's will is always expressed in a concrete situation, for a particular person in a peculiar set of circumstances at a certain time, and that it is a Christian's responsibility to discover God's will and respond to it.

This view of marriage as a vocation holds that two persons may be attracted to each other, but they will not permit themselves to be so overwhelmed by falling in love that they do not consider anything else. Instead, their love for each other will lead a Christian couple to consider carefully every aspect of their relationship—physical, emotional, social, and economic, as well as religious. In preparing for marriage they will use every appropriate resource, such as medical or financial advice, as well as premarital counseling by their minister.

How can you help couples to be aware of God's call to them? How can you help them to use the needed resources to sort out God's will for them?

A Covenant Relationship

Christian marriage is not simply a personal choice by two individuals. It is not merely a legal contract or a social institution. Nor is it just a Christian ceremony prescribed by the church. It is all of these and more. Essentially, the Methodist church understands Christian marriage "to be a covenant relationship of a man and a woman under God in which the partners live together in love and fidelity to this covenant with God." Christians believe that God's creative and redemptive love is the basis on which all human relationships should be established. The love and faithfulness seen in God's covenant with Israel and Jesus Christ are the models for these relationships. Christian marriage, then, is primarily a covenant relationship between equals, which combines the three essential elements of the personal, social, and sacred.

For you, what are the main elements of marriage as a covenant relationship?

The first element of the covenant relationship is *personal*. For the Christian, marriage originates in the call of God to particular individuals. Responding to God, two persons enter the marriage relationship on the basis of free and equal consent. There can be no coercion of any kind. The covenant relationship is based on the personal choice of two people responding to God's will for them.

Another essential element of the covenant relationship is *social*. Although personal and private in origin, marriage can never be a private association regulated only by the personal desires of two individuals. Social responsibility is intrinsic to every marriage; for good or ill, society's welfare is involved in every marriage. In our culture we recognize that marriage is a social institution having such profound effect on the total social structure that society has a right to regulate it for the common good.

The public character of Christian marriage is attested to by the fact that a couple enter into the covenant relationship in the presence of the congregation. Moreover, the Christian community is concerned enough to provide the kind of preparation for marriage that will help couples discover, and live by, God's will for them, not only within their marriage, but also in the world, as they endeavor to fulfill their common discipleship.

The third element of the covenant relationship is its *sacred* nature. The sacredness of marriage is witnessed to by the fact that it is instituted in a religious ceremony before the Christian community. That the man and the woman make the same vows attests to our belief in equality in marriage. Important also is that in Christian marriage two persons make a lifelong commitment to each other in the presence of God. They seek to be faithful to the divine model of steadfast love that comes from God. Further, God is not some external attachment added to the wedding ceremony against the will of the participants. Rather, God enters the marriage in and through the lives of the partners. To sum up, before God they make an unconditional covenant with each other to live in steadfast love and to be faithful to each other and to their vows.

A Mutual Ministry

In Christian marriage there is both the covenant (as commitment) and the relationship (as living in love and fidelity). The couple enters the covenant in the marriage ceremony, but they fulfill it in their daily relationship. The relationship is a quality of living which is in process of being realized throughout the years of their life together.

In this covenant relationship husbands and wives perform a mutual ministry of self-giving; they accept each other for better or for worse, and they enter into a new kind of "belonging" to each other. Although marriage is not considered a sacrament in The United Methodist Church, it does have a sacramental character. For God not only is in the origin and institution of the marriage, but also is a constant source of strength and guidance throughout the covenant relationship.

A Christian couple will continue in marriage, we believe, not simply because of the external pressures of society or the internal personal satisfactions, but essentially because they affirm marriage as a sacred covenant relationship based on Christian love and fidelity.

We do not mean that a man and woman are bound to maintain an empty form of marriage after all life and spirit have gone out of it. Instead, we mean that to the best of their ability a couple will contribute to the growth and enrichment of their relationship so that it continues to bless their lives, and the lives of others whom they influence. (For some of the opportunities that the church has to help couples enhance their marriages, see suggestions in chap. 4.)

We should note here that the spirit does not go out of a marriage all at once. Rather, it is apt to be a process of slow death with many danger signals along the way. As their counseling minister you can help couples see that they have an obligation to be alert to these danger signals and to react to them constructively. You can urge them to do their best to work out difficulties with understanding and love, and to allow the redemptive grace of God to work in their individual lives and in their relationship.

What do you believe God intends for couples in terms of their experiencing growth and enrichment in their marriage? When serious problems arise, how do you see God working in the lives of a couple?

A Channel for God's Love

As a husband and wife respond to the grace and love of God, we believe their marriage is opened to infinite possibilities. Nevertheless, they are still human; and it is fairly certain that they will continue to have problems. But now they can face their difficulties with a new spirit and a new power. We have discovered that, under the ministry of the Holy Spirit, couples can experience their marriage relationship as a channel for God's healing love.

The fact that husbands and wives have been redeemed does not mean that they are thereby made perfect. They are still limited human creatures who need to grow in grace and love. Unless they permit God to continue to work in their lives and relationship, they will regress. Our life is potential; we always remain open to both demonic and divine possibilities. Progress toward perfection never comes automatically for the individual or the couple. But it does come to those who open their lives to God and respond in obedient love; to those who try to enhance their relationship.

As pastors we must be realistic, however, and recognize that even redeemed persons will have many problems that must be faced and overcome. A Christian marriage, for example, is not one in which there are no problems, but one in which committed Christians are trying to find constructive solutions to problems as they arise. This means that husbands and wives always need to be open to the inspiration of the Holy Spirit. Together, they need to cooperate fully with God in changing that which causes difficulties in their lives and hinders the full expression of divine love through them. Indeed, they may discover that some of their greatest growth comes out of crisis situations.

The very fact that married couples still know themselves to be sinful human creatures who have experienced God's redeeming love before, encourages them to confess their sins, to accept again God's forgiving love, and to follow God's guidance for the future. When they do, God enables them to express forgiving love to those who have wronged them and enables them to accept the forgiving love extended by their partners. Further, because they have experienced God's grace before and trust God to be at work for wholeness, they find the strength to face their problems and to do their best to solve them.

Under the guidance of God's spirit, husbands and wives are enabled to take a patient and generous attitude toward their marriage partners. Without being unrealistic they can see their partners in terms of their highest possibilities and be optimistic about their future. We know that God works toward overcoming conflict and achieving reconciliation, that God guides and empowers persons to seek solutions to their problems. On the other hand, when they are unable to handle their problems on their own, they can be encouraged to seek competent help from an appropriate qualified source. Above all, couples need to be encouraged to allow God's spirit to work to restore their lives and relationships and to make them whole again.

When couples respond positively to the stimula-tion of God's spirit, we find that marriage becomes a channel for the expression of God's steadfast love—unconditional, sacrificing, forgiving, sustaining, affirming love. Under the influence of God's love, the events of everyday family life, in prosperity or adversity, become a "means of grace" to help persons to "go on to perfection." We do not mean that persons become perfect in the sense of being free from sin or the problems of everyday life. What we mean is that they "grow in grace" so that they seek to become "perfect in love." This is a constant seeking to let God's steadfast love find full expression in all their relationships—within their marriage and with the whole family of God. In all their relationships they are aware that God is the source of their love, that God is at work in and through them.

With all these beliefs about the worth of marriage, how do you keep from making an idol of Christian marriage?

The more we become aware of God's love at work within us and our marriage, the more we realize that marriage is not the ultimate good. Marriage is important, to be sure. But its importance is in the fact that it is a structure of life God has instituted for the benefit of persons. For this reason, we see Christian marriage as a means of helping persons develop to their fullest potential. It is also a way of supporting and enabling persons to be in service in the world.

The ultimate value in this life is always God's will and never a human relationship. The claims of the kingdom transcend those of marriage. The Christian faith affirms marriage, but limits its significance.

Such an understanding of the significance of marriage keeps us from making an idol of this relationship, important as it is. It prevents us from believing that marriage is the most sacred thing in the world, or that our highest purpose in this life is to live for our partner. It reminds us to keep marriage within the context of the reign of God in the world, so that God's will is always supreme, both in the life of the individual and in the life of the couple.

How do you integrate your theology of marriage into your practice of helping couples prepare for marriage? How do you help couples clarify their understandings of Christian marriage?

In the next chapter we describe some procedures for group preparation for marriage.

In this chapter we want to share some suggestions with you for bringing together several engaged couples to enrich their relationships. We see group preparation as a part of the premarital program that offers great possibilities for a couple's growth, learning, and understanding of their relationship. This is not intended as a substitute for your premarital counseling, but as an adjunct to it.

Following is the text of a leaflet[1] you may want to revise to fit your church and distribute to your couples. Afterwards, we will describe each module mentioned in the leaflet, and then a few others.

Your Marriage

Your marriage is important to your church. No doubt you want your marriage to be happy and fulfilling. Growing a good marriage takes a lot of work as well as a lot of love. Your church wants to help you develop the skills and understandings for a satisfying marriage. Your church and your pastor take seriously our responsibility for helping you prepare for marriage.

To assist you in this exciting adventure, your church offers a six-part program of marriage preparation. Couples planning to be married in our church are expected to take part in the entire series, unless it is impossible because of some unusual circumstances. We believe you will find it helpful to take advantage of each part of this program. Three of these come before the rehearsal and the wedding and two afterwards.

To schedule the events in your marriage preparation, contact your pastor as soon as you are engaged, whether formally or informally. We hope we can have at least six months for these events.

1. You are invited to join one of the marriage preparation groups. One of these is a Premarital Communication Lab. The lab focuses mainly on enhancing your relationship through improving your communication skills, strengthening your positive ways of relating and discovering your potentials for growth. It combines sharing information about a variety of marital concerns and experiential learning through skill practices.

Our church has one of these labs each year, usually in late April or early May. We meet at the church all day on two Saturdays from 9 a.m. to 10 p.m. This lab is open to engaged couples in the community as well as those in our church. Register as soon as possible by calling the church.

Another marriage preparation group is more informal. It is a Couples' Sharing Group. It is composed of two or three couples about to be married meeting with an equal number of married couples. In these groups you will have an opportunity to study "live human documents" by asking the married couples about any area of their marriage you wish. They will not try to tell you what to do, but they will be glad to share with you what they have learned from their life together. These groups are set up as needed throughout the year, so call the church to enroll.

2. You are invited also to read and discuss with your partner some books on preparing for marriage. Several are listed on the back of this folder.[2] One book all couples are expected to read is Preparing for Christian Marriage, *a manual on preparing for marriage. Your personal copy is available from your pastor. We will use the Premarital Questionnaires in it and refer to it frequently in your premarital counseling sessions.*

The other books are available from our church library. Any of these may be checked out for a week at a time. As your pastor I can suggest specific books if you like. We believe you will find that this reading stimulates you to talk about many areas of marital adjustment important to you.

3. Remember to contact your pastor as soon as you decide to get married so we can schedule your premarital counseling sessions. The basic plan calls for two interviews for you as a couple. It also provides a session for each of you separately. But we will decide together the exact number of sessions when we meet the first time.

The purpose of these sessions is for us to get better acquainted and to discuss any concerns you might have about any area of marriage. Some of these may grow out of your reading, your group preparation, or your own discussions with one another.

Other couples say these sessions have been very helpful to them. I know I look forward to getting to know both of you better and to sharing with you in this very significant experience in your life.

4. Your church also has some special ways of helping you with both the rehearsal and your wedding. Our plan is to conduct the rehearsal in such a way that you can be more relaxed and confident about your part in the wedding. In this way all of us can be prepared to make your wedding a high moment for you—a time of worship and dedication as you celebrate entering into the covenant relationship of Christian marriage.

Again, I urge you to call the church early so, hopefully, we can give you your first choice of dates, and get these important events on our church calendar.

Two other parts of your preparation for marriage come after your wedding.

5. From one to six months after your wedding, I would like for you to call me for your last appointment in our counseling sessions. As your pastor I want to continue to work with you in making the most of your marriage. And after you have been married for a while and have had time to experience some of the joys and struggles of marriage, you are likely to have additional concerns for us to talk over.

As you might guess, we continue this practice because other couples have indicated that this continuing contact has been valuable to them. I believe you will find it beneficial as well.

6. After you have been married about a year, we want you to take part in one of our marital growth groups. These groups are of two kinds. One is called a Marriage Enrichment Retreat.[3] It meets on a weekend in a retreat setting. The other is a Marital Support Group.[4] It meets monthly in the home of one of the couples in the group.

The Marriage Enrichment Retreat is an intensive experience designed to strengthen and enhance your marriage. We work on such marital issues as improving communication, strengthening identity and deepening intimacy, enriching our sexual life, making creative use of conflict, deepening our spiritual life, and setting goals for growth. Each retreat involves eight or ten couples plus two leader couples. We usually schedule two of these retreats each year. Dates, cost, and other information are available from the church office.

After the retreat you will be invited to join one of our Marital Support Groups. Each group is composed of four or five couples. They join together to support each other in their commitment to a growing marriage. The monthly meetings are informal, combining some social activities and marital growth experiences. These Marital Support Groups meet for about six months before regrouping.

No doubt this sounds like a full program, and you may be wondering if you can work all of this into your busy schedule. Yes, growing a good marriage does take time and effort! And your church is committed to helping you make the very best preparation possible for your marriage.

After you've been through this program, I believe you will find it worth the effort. I look forward to working with you in this important venture.

Be sure to call me as soon as you decide to get married, or before, if you have any questions.

Your Pastor,

_____

Phone _____

P.S.: *If you are moving to another community, I urge you to contact the church there and join as soon as possible. Let them know about your interest in marital growth. I believe you are likely to find the pastor there eager to get to know you and to help you in any way possible. Let me know if you plan to move so I can help you contact your new pastor.*

Models Described

We will briefly describe the models in the leaflet and several other models.

A Premarital Communication Lab

First, the Premarital Communication Lab is a model based on the Marriage Communication Lab,[5] which we originated in the early 1960s.

The Premarital Communication Lab develops a special kind of Christian community. It provides engaged couples with an opportunity to enrich their present and future relationships by improving their communication skills and using them in selected areas of marital adjustment.

This model has many values and advantages over "talking about" the adjustments anticipated in marriage, for such a lab is experiential—a living of the faith, a searching for God's will. The lab deals with the couples' (including the leader couples') present relationships and helps them improve their practices in decision-making and problem-solving. The focus is on enriching their relationships as they *experience* God's love through each other and the other members of the lab.

A Premarital Communication Lab is an *experience* in which a small group of couples, under the guidance of trained and experienced leader couples, help one another to grow in understanding; of themselves and of each other, how they affect one another, and ways they may enrich their relationships. In such a lab, couples have an opportunity to become aware of the ways they are relating, to discover both the strengths and weaknesses in their relationships, and to decide on new directions for future growth both individually and together.

The *purpose* of a Premarital Communication Lab is to help engaged couples make the best possible preparation for a sound, satisfying, growing marriage. It is not therapy, nor is it a substitute for premarital counseling. But it does have the potential for preventing problems and for preparing couples to face problems constructively when they do arise.

The *content* of a Premarital Communication Lab is the participating couples—their relationships, experiences, and feelings about the ways they are relating to one another; their growing awareness of each other's needs and desires; their expectations of each other; and their anxieties and hopes for their future together. These may be explored through considering such topics as: what is happening in our relationship, improving communication, finding sexual fulfillment in marriage, marital role expectations, enhancing identity and intimacy, facing conflicts constructively, expressing negative and positive feelings, deepening our spiritual life, and setting goals for growth in our marriage.

A variety of *methods* may be used to help couples enrich their engagement and prepare for marriage. These may include having couples talk with one another alone or in a small group; having one couple help another couple in skill training; having a "fishbowl" with men silently observing women (and vice versa) as they discuss a marital issue; or having men and women work in separate groups and report to the total group.

These methods may involve verbal and non-verbal techniques of communication such as making collages, drawing pictures, and feeding one another, or experiencing one-way communication by using wooden blocks. Other experiences may include reacting to films and tapes, sorting marital role cards, fantasizing, or being challenged and inspired by worship experiences. In this setting, several things can happen:

1) Couples can experience a sense of trust in the context of Christian community, and as a result, become more aware of the Holy Spirit as they open themselves to each other and to the group.
2) Couples discover they can be closer as they share with each other their strengths and their concerns.
3) The group experience helps break "the marital taboo" (which says couples do not talk with anyone else about their relationship) and enables couples to get help from each other.
4) The lab can promote growth. The interaction is dynamic as couples discover their potential.
5) The partners are helped to be realistic about the

expectations they bring to the relationship and to share them with each other.

6) Couples experience fun and fellowship together.

7) The emphasis of the lab is on the couple's setting goals in their relationship and recognizing that God's strength can enable them to reach their potential.

The Premarital Communication Lab requires trained leadership and should not be attempted without it.[6] One leader couple can work with up to five engaged couples. Two leader couples are needed for eight or ten engaged couples. We strongly recommend that several local churches cooperate in holding a Premarital Communication Lab.

Please note that such a lab is preferably a 48-hour weekend in a retreat setting. However, for practical reasons, we presented it above in the "Your Marriage" leaflet as occurring on two Saturdays.

The Saturday schedule, with meals and snacks provided, might look something like this:

First Saturday

9:00 a.m.	—Orientation, Getting Acquainted
12:00 noon	—Lunch
1:00 p.m.	—Improving Communication: Presentation and Practice
4:00 p.m.	—Fellowship, Browsing at Book Table, Couple Time
5:30 p.m.	—Supper
6:30 p.m.	—Enhancing Identity and Intimacy
9:30 p.m.	—Worship, Fellowship, Refreshments

(Homework: Marital Role Expectations)

Second Saturday

9:00 a.m.	—Review Marital Role Expectations
	—Learning to Express Negative and Positive Feelings
12:00 noon	—Lunch
1:00 p.m.	—Finding Sexual Fulfillment (Film)
3:00 p.m.	—Break for Couple Time
3:30 p.m.	—Using Conflict Constructively
5:30 p.m.	—Couple Time
6:00 p.m.	—Supper
7:00 p.m.	—Setting Goals for Growth in Our Marriage
9:30 p.m.	—Closing Celebration and Evaluation
	—Fellowship and Refreshments

A Couples' Sharing Group

What we describe below is an informal group experience—a Couples' Sharing Group. It is a way of tapping the resources that we believe are available to any congregation. We urge you not to try to do all of the premarital preparation yourself. Instead, we think you have people in your church who can carry a large part of the load.

While working with ACME a few years ago, we experimented with a small, informal group of couples. We asked three committed married couples of different ages to share their marriages with three engaged couples. The campus minister at Wake Forest University secured the engaged couples with whom he was doing premarital counseling. For the married couples, we chose one who had been married only about two years and had no children, one married six or seven years with two children, and we were the couple who were grandparents. All of the married couples were chosen because they had attended a marriage enrichment weekend and were open in sharing their marriages with others.

The six couples were asked to meet for two to three hours on two evenings. It was to be a very informal discussion with refreshments. The plan was for the married couples to share their marriages with the young couples by inviting them to ask the married couples anything they wanted to about their marriages. The married couples were to reserve the right to "pass" if they chose. (Actually, this never happened.) There was to be no "telling" the young couples what to do.

When the group met on the first evening the married couples responded informally to questions. Then they asked if they might ask the engaged couples about their relationships. They readily agreed. So there was a free give-and-take exchange in which all couples learned from each other. At the end of the second evening, one of the engaged persons remarked to the married couples, "You caused us to ask questions we didn't know we had."

As they started to leave, one young woman said, "We would like another evening together. We need to talk more about sex. Can we meet again next week?" Of course, the answer was "Yes!"

We all evaluated this as a good learning experience for both the married and the to-be-married couples. At the last minute one of the engaged couples had to drop out because of illness. So we ended up with two engaged couples and three married couples. That worked out all right. But we think it is best to have the same number of engaged and married couples.

We highly recommend this informal group model

and urge you to try it. Think of the ongoing support system such a plan could initiate within your church, as these couples see themselves as ministers to each other and witness through sharing their relationships.

Perhaps the way to start preparing for this kind of informal group preparation is for you and your spouse to get into a marital growth group along with several of the strongest couples in your congregation. Such a marital growth group needs to be one in which couples learn to be open in sharing their marriages with other couples. They do this by working on developing areas of their own relationships while receiving help from other couples in the process. A Marriage Communication Lab provides this opportunity.

Group Reading/Exploring

Probably most of your couples will prefer to do their reading alone or only with the person they are about to marry. But some couples may appreciate your putting them in touch with another couple who are also preparing for marriage so that they might get together to discuss some of their reading. We think it's a good idea for one couple to help another couple work through the "Explore" sections in the couple's workbook, *Preparing for Christian Marriage*.

Some couples may want you to help them contact couples who have been happily married for several years. They may want to check these couples' experience of marriage against ideas they found in the premarital books. This is a good way to help a younger couple find "adult guarantors" for their marriage. And such a relationship may be rewarding for both couples. We have found it so!

We urge you to consider the above programs very seriously. However, in addition to them—or instead of, if you prefer—there are also several other very good models.

Some of these are commercially produced, and may be purchased. Others you may develop in your church, using the resources in your congregation and community.

Couples Communication Program

We think one of the best programs is the Couples Communication Program.[7] Basically, it is a 12-hour course in communication skill training. It is not structured to deal with specific marital issues, but mainly with communication skills. Once these skills are learned, the couples can use them with any area of their relationships they wish.

Originally called the Minnesota Couples Communication Program, it was developed first as a premarital program, but has since expanded considerably. It is one of the most carefully researched programs we know. For a brief description, see chapter 16 in Herbert A. Otto's *Marriage and Family Enrichment*.

A Premarital Clinic

The premarital clinic is a structured program that may be largely information-giving through prepared presentations. In addition, the group discussions following each presentation can be occasions for individuals and couples to deal with their own attitudes, beliefs, and values.

The leadership comes primarily from the community. If you are in a rural church, you may want to invite resource people from nearby areas. We suggest that you ask an engaged couple and a married couple to join you in becoming a planning committee. In some churches there is a family council that has a subcommittee on marital growth. This might be the group to set up the planning committee. Again, we are urging you not to try to do it all, but to see that qualified persons do the planning.

This plan calls for four or five two-hour weekly sessions, depending on the issues decided upon by the committee (it might be scheduled all on one day or on a Friday night and most of a Saturday).

The following is an outline of what one church did. All sessions were held at the church in the young adults' classroom. After thirty- to forty-minute presentations, the group was encouraged to ask questions and to share in the discussions that followed.

First session—Introduction: "What Is Marriage All About?"
  Led by a minister trained in family life education. An exploration of the meaning of Christian marriage as a covenant relationship and as a Christian vocation.
Second Session—"My Body/Myself"
  Led by a medical doctor. Information about the physical aspects of marriage as a part of the total relationship. Included general health as well as birth control information.

Third Session—"What Does the Law Say?"
Led by a lawyer. A look at the legal aspects of marriage (the marriage license, income tax, property, insurance, wills, etc.).

Fourth Session—"Being Me and Being Married"
Led by a psychotherapist. Helping couples look at the personal and emotional adjustments in marriage.

Fifth Session—"And What Does It Cost?"
Led by a home economist. Focused on decisions regarding earning and spending family income, as well as suggestions for planning a budget.

The schedule for the premarital clinic can provide time for fellowship for the couples and perhaps an opportunity for them to establish new friendships with others soon to be married.

A Weekend Retreat

Again planning is done by a committee who will take responsibility for securing leadership, setting a date, finding a site, and personally contacting engaged couples to be invited (though the retreat should be open to any, of course). Here you may want to contact other churches in the area to enlist their own couples, especially if your church membership is small.

This is a more concentrated event and allows time for group building through the sessions as well as through recreational activities.

The leadership is important. The leader couples can serve as models for the participants. Perhaps you can think of two or three married couples in your congregation who could effectively share their own continuing pilgrimage.

A suggested schedule might look like this:

Friday
6:00 p.m.—Registration and room assignments
6:30 p.m.—Dinner
7:30 p.m.—Opening worship, orientation, and getting acquainted.
8:00 p.m.—"The Nature of Christian Marriage"
9:15 p.m.—Break
9:30 p.m.—"Understanding Myself and My Background—What I Bring to Marriage"
10:30 p.m.—Recreation and refreshment
11:15 p.m.—Informal closing worship

Saturday
8:00 a.m.—Breakfast
9:00 a.m.—Brief morning worship with group singing
9:30 a.m.—"Communication in Marriage"— Including Constructive Use of Conflict
11:00 a.m.—Break
11:15 a.m.—"Companionship and Compatibility"
12:30 p.m.—Lunch
1:30 p.m.—"Sexual Fulfillment in Marriage"
3:00 p.m.—Free time for hiking, swimming, volleyball, etc.
6:30 p.m.—Dinner
7:30 p.m.—"Defining Our Roles in Marriage"
8:45 p.m.—Break
9:00 p.m.—"Relationships with Parents-in Law"
10:15 p.m.—Recreation and refreshments
11:15 p.m.—Closing devotions

Sunday
8:00 a.m.—Breakfast
9:00 a.m.—Morning worship, group singing
9:30 a.m.—"Beyond Ourselves—Relationships with Friends, Community, World"
10:45 a.m.—Break
11:00 a.m.—"Spiritual Growth as a Couple"
12:30 p.m.—Dinner
1:30 p.m.—Pack and be ready to leave (This helps participants be more attentive for the afternoon session)
2:00 p.m.—Couples evaluate "Our Next Steps in Preparing for Marriage"
2:45 p.m.—Closing worship and goodbyes

We have described several kinds of group preparation, hoping that one of them will seem appropriate for you and your couples.

Beyond the inherent value of engaged couples' working in group settings, we suggest additional benefits. Involving resource people and married couples from your congregation can mean that the church shares with you in this important ministry. It can mean that participating married couples find their own marriages enriched, and therefore, that marriage as an institution is strengthened. Finally we see the potential for developing a continuing support system (a Christian community!) among the engaged or the newly-married couples and the committed married couples who share leadership.

What other ways can you think of that your congregation might help your couples prepare for marriage? Do not think only of the professionals, such as a medical doctor or a financial expert, but include the persons whose lives exhibit courage, strength, and vitality. Include the young and the old, the married and the divorced and the widowed.

Where can these persons help? When? How? When you have brainstormed on this, how about checking out members of your congregation, involving them in being the "family of families," inviting them to share their ideas of how they can help educate couples for marriage in the present and in the future, and helping the congregation be a caring Christian community.

At first glance perhaps this might seem like a lot of work, but what we are suggesting is that you enlist your people—the caring Christian community—to share with you in this life-changing ministry, that they may be in ministry, too.

Whether in group preparation or in individual and couple counseling, premarital preparation has certain purposes and content. This is the subject of the next part of this book.

Chapter 5
Marriage and Self-Understanding

In addition to the overall purpose of helping a couple prepare for marriage, what specific goals do you want to achieve in working with them either separately or in a group?

If you are sure about your purposes, and have them fairly clear in your own mind, you will be able to move into preparing couples for marriage with more confidence and with a sense of direction.

Six goals are suggested here: (1) to help the couple understand the nature of marriage, interpreted, of course, in the light of the Christian faith; (2) to enable each partner to understand himself or herself and what each brings to marriage as a person; (3) to guide the couple in being realistic about the adjustments they must make in marriage; (4) to help them discover their strengths and weaknesses and what additional guidance and resources they need; (5) to stimulate and often to educate couples in effective communication; and (6) to establish or strengthen a pastoral relationship with the couple. Implicit in these purposes are two others—helping the couple to set goals for continuing growth and helping them to evaluate their relationship and readiness for marriage (these two are dealt with in Part III).

These goals are not separate items to be worked on one at a time. They are very closely interrelated and will overlap considerably as you work on them. They are stated separately here for explanation and emphasis. Nor are they listed in the order of their importance; for establishing or strengthening a pastoral relationship with a couple may be your first purpose. Unless this is accomplished, you can do very little to achieve the other goals.

What other goals do you think should be added?

The first two goals listed above are discussed in this chapter. A full chapter is devoted to each of the other four.

Your overall aim is to make available to the couple(s)—sometimes in a group or individually, but mostly as a couple—some specific help in their preparation for marriage. We believe that each of these areas is important and should be given some attention, and be explored in depth according to the needs of the individual couples.

Begin Where They Are

In helping two persons comprehend the nature of marriage, we believe it is important for you to begin where they are in their understanding. Nevertheless, you will have in mind certain concepts that you consider essential to a Christian interpretation of marriage. You also have responsibility to yourself as the one who must decide whether or not you will marry a particular couple.

To begin where they are, it may be necessary to start with the wedding rather than with the marriage. The couple may come wanting to prepare for the wedding, an event, rather than for their relationship. They may have many questions about the rehearsal or the reception as well as the ceremony itself. (Some churches—through worship commissions and the administrative boards—have developed a policy statement covering questions about decorations, music, picture-taking, fees, and so forth, so as to protect and enhance the worshipful nature of the service. You may want to have such a statement in printed form to give to each couple.) In the back of the couple's workbook, you will find a Wedding Information blank, which will help answer these questions.

We believe it will be more productive to begin with the couple's immediate concerns. Their questions need to be handled with care. If you will deal with their questions directly and effectively, they are apt to feel that you care about *them*, too. One of the primary aims of the initial interview is to establish a relationship of warmth and trust that will facilitate free and open sharing.

With couples who want to prepare their own ceremony, you may have the opportunity of guiding them in designing a worship service that focuses on, and celebrates, the values they have discovered in their exploration of the meaning of Christian marriage.

You may want to explore the couple's understanding of marriage in relation to the concepts of monogamy, vocation, covenant relationship, and other elements of a Christian marriage.

As soon as the couple is ready, you will want to *help them review their understanding* of the nature of marriage and guide them in evaluating this understanding in the light of the Christian faith (in the previous chapter you will find some background material that may be helpful to you at this point).

The first concept to discuss is our belief that marriage is a *lifelong union of a man and a woman, based on love and loyalty*. Do both partners intend their marriage to last "till death us do part"?

Do they know what it means to "forsake all other" and "keep thee only unto him (or her)"? Most couples respond rather quickly to this, saying that this means sexual fidelity. But very few relate it to the scriptural account in Genesis 2:24. "Therefore a man leaves his father and his mother and cleaves to his wife, and they become one flesh." They may need some help in shifting their primary loyalty from their family of origin to the new union they are establishing.

Do they understand that both love and fidelity are essential foundations of marriage? Does their understanding of love include a positive attitude toward sex? These and other questions may help clarify their understanding of the nature of marriage.

The term *Christian vocation* applied to marriage may be new to most couples. But they are likely to know what is meant by entering marriage as a result of a deliberate choice, rather than drifting into marriage. However, they probably will need help in evaluating their decision in the light of God's will for them. How do they discover God's will? How do they know they are responding to God's call to marriage? To be sure, these are questions that are easy to ask and hard to answer. But they need to be faced.

What does it mean to the couple to talk about marriage as *a covenant relationship*? Are they prepared to fulfill each part of this commitment? What is the significance to them of an unconditional covenant with each other before God? Are they committing themselves, not only to a lifelong union, but also to growing in love, to a continuing effort to achieve a quality relationship? This quality relationship, we believe, also should be one of *equality*. In a covenant relationship we see the recognition of the infinite worth of each partner as a unique individual created by God.

Other elements that may be considered in connection with a Christian understanding of the nature of marriage are at least five practical, yet deeply spiritual, concerns. One is the *personal commitment* to God as revealed in Jesus Christ. Another is the ability to give and receive *genuine love*. Ideally, this is self-giving love—sacrificing, forgiving, sustaining, affirming love—freely given.

A third concern is the importance of their being a part of *Christian community*, being actively related to a church. A fourth is their *concern for others*, which takes them beyond their own needs and satisfactions in marriage to involvement in service to the community and world.

The fifth concern is in the area of *purposes and values*. As a couple, how do they describe the overall goal of their life together? How is this related to God's will for them as they understand it? What do they believe is the highest value in this life? How do they plan to realize this value as a couple? What do they believe will give the deepest meaning to their marriage? Again, the couple may have dealt with many of these concerns through using the couple's workbook.

Readiness for Marriage

In your effort to help the couple understand the nature of marriage, you also have a responsibility to yourself. You will want to assess the couple's readiness for marriage to be sure you feel justified in marrying them.[1] This is both a matter of personal integrity—being true to yourself as a minister of the gospel—and a matter of responsibility to the church and community, as well as to the couple. In the process of deciding you are helping the couple to examine their total readiness for marriage.

To meet this obligation, you need to ask yourself some questions about the couple. Without being judgmental, you can keep the questions listed below in the back of your mind as you interview the couple. Some of the questions relate to facts; others will be based on your feelings about the couple. If doubtful about some of the answers, you may require certain tests, request a series of interviews, or suggest a referral for additional help from another professional, such as a psychotherapist. After extending all the resources of the Christian faith to them, you may feel that you must refuse to marry some couples.

The following questions may help in the screening process:

Are legal requirements being met or violated: license, age or consent of parents, health test, waiting period? Are your own church requirements being met or ignored?

Do these persons give frivolous or serious reasons for wanting to get married?

Are they entering marriage freely or under duress?

Are they mature enough mentally and emotionally to understand the meaning of the vows and give reasonable promise of fulfilling them?

Do they give indications that they intend to fulfill their marriage vows, or do they seem to take them too lightly?

Are there any serious mental, emotional, physical, or other handicaps that might endanger their marriage? Have these been adequately understood, accepted, and dealt with insofar as possible?

Is there such marked personality incompatibility that psychological testing is indicated?

Are there differences in age, background, values, and so forth, which will enrich or threaten their relationship?

If this is a second marriage, has sufficient time elapsed since the death or divorce for the person to have overcome the hurt and made adequate preparation for the new marriage?

Is the couple willing to follow through with the premarital preparation so that any questions can be checked out further or actually dealt with through the sessions?

Just as a marriage counselor finds it necessary to evaluate a couple's ability to use counseling before proceeding too far into the process, we hope you will assess a couple's readiness for marriage tentatively at first, and review this assessment as the interviews progress.

We urge you to plan for an evaluation for you and the couple before the end of the premarital preparation. This should be made clear early in the counseling. Such an evaluation can provide helpful feedback both to you and to the couple. It also provides the opportunity for you to share your perceptions with them.

If at the time of the evaluation you have real questions about the marriage's working, these need to be raised. If trust has been built, these concerns can be shared non-judgmentally, out of a sense of genuine caring.

Of course, you are not responsible for making the decision for the couple to marry or not to marry. They always have the option of going to someone else. But you do have responsibility for *yourself*, as stated earlier. We pose several questions for you to ask yourself:

Can *I* perform this ceremony? If not, will they marry anyway, and who will do it? What effect will my refusal have on the couple's relationship to me? To the church? What will the couple gain or lose, if I decide not to marry them?

If I decide to go ahead and marry them, what will I be saying to them? What will I be saying about myself? My theology? My role as pastor? What do *I* hope to gain? What do I expect to happen to this couple? Should *I* consider asking them to continue in counseling after they are married?

These are difficult questions. For us, the primary guideline is caring about the couple and their future. If the couple decide to marry even when your best judgment says it may not work, we believe your being there for them and establishing a pastoral relationship will keep you available to them if they should need you later.

Self-Understanding

Another major purpose of premarital preparation is to enable each partner to understand himself or herself and what each partner brings to marriage as a person. At times this may be done in groups, but more likely it will happen in the counseling sessions, especially in the individual interviews.

Such understanding may be a growth experience for the individual. In the premarital preparation you attempt to help each person appreciate what he or she brings to marriage: style of life, philosophy, attitudes and values; temperament and personality characteristics, as these have developed out of the individual's unique family, religious, educational, social, and economic backgrounds.

In this whole area of self-understanding, you will need to weigh carefully just how much it is possible to do with each person who comes to you. It is important to work within the limits of the person's readiness as well as the limits of your expertise and the time available. What is presented here, therefore, is not what every pastor should attempt to accomplish with every person in premarital preparation. Instead, it is a discussion of some aspects of your working with those who evidence special needs and who are willing to take the time to explore them in depth.

Undoubtedly the chief emphasis in the planning for marriage is on the relationship between the persons who are getting married, for each one makes a unique contribution to the marriage. Self-understanding is therefore one of the major purposes of premarital preparation.

Premarital counseling *is not individual therapy*, but it does involve helping persons become aware of what they, as individuals, bring to marriage. You will have to decide just how far to go in this area with each individual. With some you may feel that almost no help is needed. You may feel that others need extended counseling or should be referred for personal therapy. In either case, you need to make such decisions on the basis of a careful evaluation.

The basic approach in this area, as in other areas of marriage preparation, is one in which you assist individuals in discovering who they are and in developing a more adequate appreciation of themselves as individuals. Your task is not to tell them what they need. When referral is indicated, however, it is your responsibility to recognize this need and to try to help the person understand the value of the additional service. Certainly it is the individual who decides whether or not to accept the referral.

In helping an individual to understand himself or herself, there are two basic considerations, *identity* and *sexuality*, which we believe underlie all the others. Here are some issues and questions that may stimulate your thinking about the significance of these considerations in relation to marriage.

The ancient admonitions to "know thyself," "accept thyself," "be thyself" may seem like oversimplifications. But they identify some things that are basic to healthy personality development; that is, *self-understanding, self-acceptance, and being one's true self*. To what extent do the individuals you are working with evidence these qualities? Have they worked through the identity crisis?[2] Do they know who they are as persons? Have they a clear understanding of themselves as individuals in relation to others? Do they understand themselves as members of the groups out of which they come? (This is why family, ethnic group, race, and nationality are significant.) Have they a healthy acceptance of this background? What kind of accommodations are they making to various aspects of their backgrounds? Do they reject some elements? What is the meaning of these rejections? Have they the inner strength to work through these reformulations of character? Is the person growing stronger in this reshaping of the self, or is the ego strength being threatened or weakened by the struggle?

Chapter 2 in the couple's workbook includes a number of experiments to help the couple be aware of the backgrounds, attitudes, and beliefs that have contributed to who they are.

How one feels about oneself as a person is also of major importance. *A strong self-respect and self-regard are important elements in an individual's psychic health. They are also important foundational elements in any wholesome relationship, especially the intimate relationship of marriage.*

A person who has a low self-estimate, who lacks a genuine self-love, will find it difficult, if not impossible, to love another person. Perhaps most people coming to you will have a fairly mature sense of self-appreciation. Some may grow considerably through experiencing full acceptance and affirmation in their relationship with you. Still others may need to be referred for more intensive counseling or therapy (see chap. 7).

When you do find a person who does not esteem himself or herself very highly, you will want to check carefully on the partner too. What is it in the partner that causes the other to be drawn to such a person?

At times the greater need for growth may be in the partner, who may give the outward appearance of being a fairly strong person, but who is inwardly so insecure that he or she needs a weaker person to be dependent upon. A marriage of such persons is likely to arrest or retard the growth potential in both partners. Such problems as these underscore the need for counseling with such individuals and for having a consultant on call for yourself whenever needed. Even though you may not need to call on this professional very often, it is reassuring to know that help is available when needed.

One aspect of being, which is very important in self-understanding and in marriage, is *a person's feelings about his or her sexuality*. This means the acceptance—preferably, the affirmation—of the fact that one is a sexual being, that one is a man or a woman and has sexual feelings (see the couple's workbook, chap. 6, on sexuality).

To what extent has the individual accepted the fact that he or she is a sexual being, and that sex feelings are normal and wholesome? Is there any rejection of these feelings? Because of cultural conditioning, many persons come to marriage with negative feelings about sex. Undoubtedly they need help in affirming sex as one of God's good gifts.

Others will need help in affirming their sexuality in the whole area of maleness and femaleness. This involves not simply their gender, but the whole matter of what it means to be a man or a woman, and the healthy acceptance of masculinity and femininity —the feeling that "I'm glad I'm a man!" or, "It's great to be a woman!"

Sexual conditioning by culture has often been damaging to both men and women. For men, the demand has been on performance with little regard for his own or his partner's feelings. For women, the message has been, "It's your duty," and "You're a lady, so don't enjoy it."

Such messages are degrading to both men and women. For the man, the internalized message is, "I'm really selfish and feel guilty about the way I treat her"; for the woman, "I'm being used, and I'm feeling like a second-class citizen."

You can help a couple see that sex is only a small (though significant) part of their sexuality; that they are always sexual beings; that their regard for each other as equals in the total relationship is integral to sexual satisfaction.

In exploring feelings about sexuality, you may discover, for example, that a person has had some homosexual experiences. (More than one-third of the men have had such contacts.) Some persons may be very much concerned about the effect of these experiences on their marriage. Some may be carrying an exaggerated feeling of guilt as the result of only one or two such contacts, which were a part of childhood or early adolescent sexual experimentation, and nothing more. A few, however, may be much more deeply troubled by an established pattern of continuing homosexual feelings and/or experiences, and may be questioning just who they are as sexual persons.

Depending on your own attitudes and skills, you may be able to counsel some of these persons. The latter group usually require more intensive counseling. In either case, we believe it is important for you to have the best information possible regarding the social scientists' findings to date.[3] Here are several examples. Approximately 37 percent of the men and 20 percent of the women have had at least one homosexual experience to the point of orgasm. About 10 percent of the population is predominately or exclusively gay—13.95 percent of the males and 4.25 percent of the females. The causes of homosexuality are unknown. One's sexual orientation is considered a discovery, not a choice. There is little evidence that even with extensive "treatment" one can "change" one's orientation.

Of course your attitude is more important than knowing the facts. Regardless of your own personal beliefs, the question is: Can you be there for the person who is dealing with these concerns? If you feel that you cannot, it will be important to acknowledge your own discomfort or uncertainty (which will be evident to the person anyway) and to make a referral.

Other areas of self-understanding may be opened up by using the Premarital Questionnaires in the back of the couple's workbook. For example, see questions 13, 31-33, and 38.

An individual frequently comes to marriage heavily loaded with intangible baggage. A person brings *his or her own philosophy of life,* interpretation of certain moral and spiritual values, particular attitudes toward people, issues, and institutions, personal views on various political and social problems, and commitments and involvements in supporting or challenging various aspects of our culture. These are some of the foundational elements of an individual's life and hence are basic to any deep and meaningful marriage relationship. If you can help a couple clarify and verbalize some of these basic positions, you may be making a fundamental contribution to a couple's future—not only to each individual's self-understanding, but also to the possibility of depth and growth in the marriage.

Each person also brings a variety of influences from *the background from which he or she comes*. (Here again, the Premarital Questionnaires and the couple's workbook, chap. 2, will be helpful.) Here are some questions for each of the partners. What kind of family did you grow up in? What was your relationship with your parents and brothers and sisters? How did your parents get along with each other? More important, how did this affect you? What is the present marital status of your parents?

What was the religious environment you grew up in? How active in church are you now? What is your educational background? Are you still in school or planning additional education? What kind of work did your father do? What is your own present occupation? Did your mother work outside the home? How did you feel about it? How much social life did you have during your teens? Since then? These are the kinds of questions that should help an individual to understand what kind of person he or she is and how important his or her background is.

One needs to understand oneself in terms of

temperament and other personal characteristics. In one way or another, one may ask: What kind of person am I? How do I affect other people? Am I concerned mainly with my own needs and pleasures, or do I care about others too? Do I express anger freely, or hold it back? Am I rigid or flexible? Am I easily influenced by others? Easily depressed or discouraged? Jealous? Punctual? And so on.

One may be helped to understand oneself better by having an opportunity to place oneself somewhere on the continuum suggested by such questions as these: What kind of temperament do I have—controlled or impulsive? Aggressive or submissive? Warm or cold? Active or quiet? Serious-minded or light-hearted? Nervous or composed? Critical or appreciative of others? These are the kinds of traits the Taylor-Johnson Temperament Analysis attempts to measure. It is highly recommended by many counselors.[4]

Still another aid to self-understanding is a summary of *a person's interests and activities:* such as various business and professional meetings, membership in certain clubs or organizations, specific hobbies, activities related to political or social concerns, creative activities, reading, social gatherings with friends, variety of outdoor activities, spectator or participatory sports, attending plays or movies, and so forth. It is instructive to know not only the activities, but also the frequency and the enjoyment of each (see question 29, Premarital Questionnaire).

Inevitably, one brings to marriage *all one's emotional needs*—personal and affectional needs, the need for companionship, the need to love and be loved. Each partner brings his or her sexual needs and desires, which must be fitted into an ongoing pattern of mutually satisfying sexual relationships; and the sometimes ambivalent needs for intimacy and privacy. Each person brings his or her ego needs, especially the need for a sense of self-worth.

Under the pressure of so many depersonalizing forces in our society today, the effort to satisfy these personal needs in marriage may place heavy demands on a partner and create a severe strain in the marriage relationship. In fact, we think couples need to maintain a sense of individuality in their marriages so that the relationship can grow rather than be stifled. What we are emphasizing is a balance between individuality and relationship. That is to say, if a couple decides to develop a relationship that is extremely close, the boundary designating the self of each partner has to be clearly defined if the self is to remain intact. Of course, finding mutual satisfaction

of these emotional needs in marriage can strengthen the relationship and give both partners a sense of well-being.

In your premarital sessions it may be appropriate for you to help some persons explore *the motivations that bring them to marriage.* Some of these may grow out of significant relationships that were unsatisfying or distorted during childhood. Marriage may be an effort to satisfy some of these basic needs, however belatedly.

In talking with you, some partners may discover that the motives that led them to choose each other were based on complementary self-fulfillment. It is as though one discovers in the other that part of oneself which is as yet unrealized. For some couples, this intermeshing of their personalities works as smoothly as hand-in-glove. For others, it creates a great deal of friction. For some this complementarity may be healthy. For others it may be an unhealthy dependency, and may call for additional professional help.

Everyone, unless severely crippled psychologically and spiritually, brings to marriage *the potential of growth.* For there is within each person a God-given drive toward health and wholeness. People can change. And they can change for the better, even though this may be difficult.

Self-understanding, in itself, is one form of growth. It also lays the foundation for future growth.

Let us say another word about growth. We believe most couples need help in understanding the nature of growth in marriage. *Change is inevitable, but growth must be intentional.* This involves risk and openness on the part of each partner. It also involves planning in the present for the future. We see setting goals for growth and implementing these goals as essential for developing a dynamic and exciting relationship.

We invite you to take time just now to assess your own growth, as an individual if you are single, or as a couple if you are married. Write down separately the ways you have grown in the past year. What were the most exciting changes for you? How purposive were you in the changes? How did you feel about each change at the time? And how do you feel about each change now?

How did you decide to make the change? Was someone else involved in the change? If so, how did that change affect your relationship? What changes would you like to make in the near future? In the distant future? What would be your next step in that direction? If you are in a relationship, share these thoughts and feelings with that person. Decide what you can do to support your partner in the growth that is desired.

Perhaps we should emphasize again, however, that preparing for marriage is not intended to be solely, or even primarily, a search for self-understanding. One of the aims is to help two persons realize and assess what it is that they bring to the marriage relationship. For the quality of that relationship will be affected strongly by what the partners bring to it. In the next chapter, we examine some of the expectations and adjustments involved in marriage.

One of our aims in preparation for marriage is to guide the couple in being realistic about the adjustments they will have to make in marriage. Many couples do not realize that they are adjusting to marriage itself, as well as to each other. But most of them do have some knowledge, however sketchy and incomplete, about some of the areas of adjustment; such as sex, finances, or family. Your purpose is to see that they are not overlooking any significant area of adjustment. You will also be concerned that they be realistic in their expectations regarding their roles as husband and wife.

One way to check on possible adjustments is the use of the Premarital Questionnaires in the back of the couple's workbook. In fact, the questions have been devised for this purpose. See especially question 38 on disagreements. Of course, other areas of agreement or disagreement may be revealed in almost every other question by comparing the responses (see page 86).

Unrealistic Expectations

Some couples approach marriage with unrealistic expectations. Their dreams of marriage are indeed romantic and illusory, unreal fantasies of impossible anticipation. In spite of much evidence to the contrary, many still look upon marriage as a cure-all.

Stimulated by our culture that is highly individualistic and pleasure-seeking, it is no wonder that so many persons think first of their own happiness and what they can get out of marriage rather than about the other person or the relationship, and the effort a good marriage requires. Nancy Friday makes a sharp distinction between this faulty sense of self which she calls "secondary narcissism," and healthy "primary narcissism." She describes secondary narcissism as being "pathological because it attempts to fill the void in the healthy self-image with an intense preoccupation with the self."[1]

Some persons are unrealistic, not only in what they expect, but in how they expect it to happen— almost automatically, without any effort on their part.

Chapter 3 of the couple's workbook provides helpful exercises for the couple to be more aware of what each partner wants and needs, and to share this with each other. We hope you will help the couple see the importance of being aware of, and sharing with each other, their expectations. You may need to help some couples negotiate how they will integrate their expectations into the marriage.

This does not mean either one's just giving up what is important to him or her, or simply giving in. Nor does it mean demanding that either one always gets what he or she wants. As we have already indicated, a healthy relationship involves two healthy persons with a sense of self-worth and integrity. They have a genuine respect for each other and a commitment to each other's good. What we are suggesting is a win-win situation where both partners, through negotiation, can feel good about the decisions they make together.

Usually couples are not totally unrealistic. Most are unrealistic about only one or two areas of adjustment. Your task is to help them identify these areas and to find ways of working on them.

On the other hand, there is an increasing number of young adults who go almost to the opposite extreme. These are the ones who have become disenchanted with anything that has a hint of the sentimental about it. They are so "realistic" about the business of marriage that they give very little place to feeling. They are so "sophisticated" that they are never swept off their feet by anything, especially not by love. They appear to be calm about almost everything.

These persons are careful about advance planning. They have everything under control. In fact, they may be so careful with their money that they cannot enjoy it. Or money may be unimportant to them, something to be used. These are the ones who want to be so successful in business that they do all the right things for the organization. They go through all the proper motions, but without much spirit.

Both the unrealistic and the overly realistic persons are likely to resist premarital preparation. The former are afraid that talking about their relationship will somehow diminish their happiness. The latter think they do not need it—they know what they are doing! Both kinds of persons need to experience your pastoral concern for their welfare and have the opportunity to test it.

The vast majority of people are somewhere between these extremes. To be sure, most of them may still approach marriage with some romantic feelings. There is nothing wrong with this, as long as it does not interfere with responsible handling of the realities of marriage. In fact, one of the aims of your working with them is to enhance the thrill and excitement of getting married and to encourage the continuation of genuine romance in marriage. The purpose is not to dull the spirit, but to throw around it the framework that will conserve and release it and increase the joy of it.

One reason why most couples approach marriage unrealistically is that *they come to it without adequate preparation.* In a sense, everything that happens to them from birth is preparing them for marriage. But some of these experiences are hurtful and may make it difficult for them to achieve the mutually satisfying adjustments required by marriage. At best, this is a hit-or-miss kind of preparation, with no organization, and sometimes little depth.

Each person comes to marriage having been exposed to particular husband-and-wife roles, and each partner's experience may be quite different. They may feel that these roles have been appropriate for their parents, but may not be suitable for couples living in today's changing world. This is especially true today with the changing expectations about marital roles.

In spite of the fact that many schools and churches are making special efforts at better preparation for marriage, particularly at the high school level, most people still come to marriage with inadequate preparation. This leaves the door open for the kind of preparation you can help them make. Even though the specific opportunity comes very late to most pastors, you can still do much to help many couples. In fact, the pre-marriage period is viewed by some as one of the most "teachable moments" in a person's life.[2]

Adjusting to Marriage

One of your primary aims, then, is to help couples realize what it means to adjust to marriage as a new state in life, as well as adjusting to each other. One area where marriage calls for changes is that of freedom and responsibility. When two persons are married, they are exchanging the freedom to act as unattached individuals for a different kind of freedom with each other. Previously they have been able to make their own decisions, often without reference to anyone else. Now, in marriage, the partner is involved in almost every decision. After the wedding, almost every move must be considered in terms of how one's mate feels about it, or how it might affect the couple's life together.

Likewise, marriage is a relationship that carries a great deal of responsibility with it. Although each of the partners is still an individual, responsible for his or her own life to a large degree, each is responsible for the relationship with the other.

Marriage means a new way of life, a new set of values and goals. It means obligations and responsibilities as well as pleasures and privileges. Many people approaching marriage do not realize the extent of these changes and may need help from you to face them.

Since marriage is such an intimate and inclusive relationship, helping partners *adjust to each other as two whole persons* is one of the most significant services of premarital preparation. The establishment of a mutually satisfying relationship is basic to the ability of each to adjust in other specific areas, such as sex or finances.

It is inevitable that some tensions, and even some open conflicts, will develop when two unique individuals come together in marriage. No matter how many interests and values they hold in common, they will have differences too. Differences arise out of the fact that they are unique individuals, and because one is a man and the other is a woman, and the culture has told them how to be! This is more than a simple matter of physical sex differences. There is also the whole matter of sexuality as maleness and femaleness, and adjusting includes their personality as well as the roles they perform (see p. 27 and Questionnaire for a marriage role expectation inventory).

In spite of much talk today about the disappearance of sexual distinctions—and some of this is happening—the fact remains that marriage partners are still a man and a woman, each with a personal approach to life. The present-day transition and confusion in sex roles creates real problems for some couples—problems of uncertainty, threat, conflict. We believe couples can make a continuing effort to understand what is happening to them and work together creatively to develop a mutually satisfying relationship.

The adjustment of two persons to each other involves the relating of all aspects of their personhood, as outlined in the above section on self-understanding. This includes *the total dynamic interacting of two whole persons.* Each partner meets the other with his or her own particular constellation of attitudes toward self and sexuality, philosophy of life and system of values, influences from the various aspects of his or her background, interests, and activities, and individual personality characteristics and emotional needs. A couple may need guidance in evaluating their own special way of interacting. Are they in basic agreement (or conflict) regarding their philosophy of life? Do they share similar value systems? At what points do they differ? How serious or superficial are these differences? Is similarity or difference in various aspects of their background—family, education, economic, social, religious—such that their relationship will be enriched or endangered? Do they have many interests in common? Do they enjoy doing the same things? To what extent is each person learning to share in the other's interests and activities?

Most emphasis, however, is usually focused on personality characteristics and emotional needs when trying to determine *compatibility.* How does each partner react to the temperament or disposition of the other? How do their personality characteristics relate? Do they clash or harmonize? Are they able to meet each other's emotional needs? If serious differences are evident, psychological testing may be indicated.[3]

Special attention may be given to the complementary theory of mate selection, mentioned briefly above. Often the very need that brings a couple together—finding fulfillment in the other—may be the thing that creates friction between them.[4]

For example, a serious-minded woman and a light-hearted man may be drawn to each other. Each needs the complementary quality of the other. When such needs mesh harmoniously, they are compatible. But this combination may be the source of conflict, especially if the woman feels that the man is not serious enough, or if he feels that she is expecting too much of him. Actually, conflict here is between their temperament needs and their role expectations.

Adjustments in Certain Areas

The most frequently used approach in helping couples to be realistic about the adjustments in marriage is probably concentration on certain areas of their relationship. Usually selected are religion, money, common interests and goals, sex, work, and in-laws.

Approximately three-fourths or more of United Methodist pastors indicate that they usually discuss these subjects with couples.[5] Here are fourteen most frequently mentioned subjects listed in order of frequency and with the percentage of pastors who discussed these subjects.

Subject	Percent
Spiritual significance of marriage	90
Religious faith of the couple	89
Meaning of the marriage ceremony	85
Money matters	80
Common interests and goals	78
Sexual relationships	75
Occupations, wife working	75
Relationships with relatives	74
Where they will live	71
Birth control and family planning	64
Desire for children by both	63
Dynamic emotional forces	55
Family backgrounds	49
Relationships with old friends	33

It is interesting to speculate as to why certain subjects are discussed much less frequently than others; for example "dynamic emotional forces." Is it because pastors consider this area of a couple's relationship less important than religion, money, or sex? Or is it because most feel less qualified to work in this area?

Thirty percent of the pastors indicated that "there are some subjects [we] feel deserve consideration," but [we] "do not feel qualified or comfortable in discussing with couples." When given the opportunity to indicate what subjects they feel uncomfortable discussing, more (15 percent) listed "sexual matters" than any other one subject. Only about 2 percent listed "dynamic emotional forces." If you believe an area deserves consideration, but feel unqualified to deal with it, we hope you will make a referral or be stimulated to professional growth on your part.

We give special attention here to three areas of adjustment as illustrations, rather than giving definitive coverage of all areas. Some pastors prefer the developmental task approach to be sure that a more comprehensive coverage is attempted (see chapter 15). Others concentrate on marital role expectations.

Religion

The discussion of religion should include, not only the spiritual significance of marriage and the meaning of the wedding ceremony (see p. 152), but also the religious faith of the couple—their beliefs and practices, their goals and purposes, their doubts and growing edges of faith. This discussion often centers around the church or faith group they belong to and the extent of their activity. If they differ on religious issues, they should discuss alternatives that they are considering adopting after marriage, and how each one feels about the various possibilities. They may be helped to explore these in depth.

Devotional readings and Bible study in the home may be encouraged, often by the suggestion or gift of a book of daily devotions. Also important is a consideration of the moral and spiritual values they share (or differ on) and how they plan to express these in their daily living.

It may be difficult not to preach a sermon at this point instead of making the consideration of religion a true experience of enabling the couple to share their religious views and questions (see p. 96).

Money

Since money is mentioned by many couples as a major cause of conflict in marriage, careful planning of finances should be encouraged. In most middle-class marriages, money problems are only the symptom of other conflicts. The real cause of conflict may be much deeper in the dynamic emotional factors of a couple's relationship. Money may be the focus of a power struggle. In some families, however, the lack of money is a root cause of problems, and conflict about it is not a symptom. This is true in the case of many younger couples, or in the case of poor families, or families in situations where employment is unstable. For most couples today, inflation makes money concerns very real.

Attitudes and feelings about money are most important and should be explored. Such exploration may uncover some surprising feelings, even for couples who think they have already agreed on how to handle their finances. It is important to get these feelings out in the open, where their meaning can be evaluated, and the couple can work on them together. *Preparing for Christian Marriage*, the couple's workbook, chapter 7, provides many thought-provoking questions that are specific and open-ended and can be used in this exploration with your couples.

From our point of view, one of your most important tasks is helping a couple to be purposive in their living, and that includes the way they choose to spend their money. Even more important is helping the couple evaluate their lifestyle in the light of their faith.

Can we help couples see that with their possessions they have a relationship to all of humankind? We think so!

We believe that as a part of the family of God we have a responsibility to the rest of the world and to what will happen to future generations. Some questions we would ask are related to the use of our natural resources, to our eating habits, and to our spending for things. These issues are critical for all of us today. No longer can we afford to be unconcerned or detached.

Sex

In talking with a couple about their sexual adjustment, you may have three aims in mind: (1) to provide the climate that will free them to talk about any sexual attitudes and practices that are important to them; (2) to encourage a Christian attitude toward sex; and (3) to make available specific information and resources in this area, according to the couple's needs.

We think *the important factor in providing the climate for the free discussion of sex is your own attitude*, being comfortable with your own sexuality. Such climate has more to do with your being the kind of person who is easy to talk with than it does with adopting any particular approach or technique. This climate is established when you are seen as a person who genuinely feels and expresses a helpful concern for persons. This is a quality of being that obviates the possibility of a judgmental or condemning attitude. You are not shocked, for example, by the report of premarital sexual practices—not because you are shielded by a thick coat of asbestos, but because your deep concern for the person affirms the personhood of the individual.

It is important not to probe into areas that a person is not ready to explore, but rather to be sensitive in catching and reflecting the true attitudes that are only hinted at in words. By this approach, the person feels understood and appreciated, and is freed to move into an examination of deeper feelings and to share any disturbing experiences.

If you feel uncomfortable in discussing certain sex matters, it is important not to exceed your own limits. Otherwise, your embarrassment or uncertainty may cause a couple to hesitate to dig into other areas at another time. It is wise to counsel within the limits of comfort. On the other hand, unless you go somewhat beyond these limits you may never enlarge the boundaries of usefulness.[6]

Within a setting of acceptance, *you will want to discern each person's attitudes*. Then you will know just how much help is needed. You will have the opportunity to encourage a positive Christian attitude, one that affirms and appreciates sex as a good gift of God, to be enjoyed and not used only, or primarily, for procreation. The Christian view also sets sexual intercourse in the context of the total interpersonal relationship of two whole persons and does not treat it solely or primarily as a physical phenomenon. Again you may find it helpful to integrate chapter 6 of the couple's workbook here.

Even though the majority of persons coming to you are likely to have had sexual intercourse, you may expect most of them—sometimes as high as three out of four—to need some help with attitudes toward sex. In spite of the sexual freedom today, past conditioning often hangs on in the form of negative attitudes, such as the belief that sex is either dirty or sinful, or that sex is not enjoyed as much by women as by men.

Also, the overemphasis on sex in our contemporary culture often fosters an exploitative attitude that is highly individualistic and self-centered pleasure-seeking, rather than the kind of pleasure-giving that nourishes companionship. Fortunately, such attitudes are improving.

Most persons approaching marriage, however, need help; and we hope you are the person who can give it. This is especially true when a person has felt used or abused in a previous marriage or in a premarital relationship. In such instances a series of individual appointments may be added to the usual pattern of interviews. The experience of discussing

sex with you in the setting of the Christian church can have a very positive effect in correcting false information or in dispelling fears.

Many persons come to marriage with *unrealistic expectations about sex*. Others have very limited knowledge and experience in this area. These are reasons why you need to make available to all couples specific guidance and resources regarding the sex adjustment in marriage.

Some persons expect too much. Sex is so glamorized in our culture that some couples admit a letdown in the actual experience of intercourse. Some think that sex is supposed to be the most important thing in marriage. Others may expect a mutually satisfying experience (including simultaneous orgasm) with first intercourse or within the first week. When their expectations are not realized, they may be very upset, or feel inadequate, or suspect that there is something seriously wrong with them, or that they may be "incompatible." They need to know in advance that it takes time—often many weeks or several months—with a lot of give-and-take, for most couples to realize a good sexual relationship.

Some will expect a perfect sexual adjustment automatically, without any special knowledge or skill or effort on their part. They come to marriage thinking they know all they need to know, when actually their knowledge may be quite limited. Many are plagued with "the myth of naturalism"—the belief that "sex comes naturally" and they do not need any help in adjusting sexually. In our experience with couples, we have found that many educated and sophisticated persons believe this to be true. For many, it is a relief to know there is not something wrong with them, and that they can learn.

How Much Help?

In this area of sex adjustment some pastors feel that they should limit their premarital counseling to a discussion of attitudes. For various reasons they feel that they should not make any references to anatomy or give any guidance in the techniques of sex relations. Most pastors, however, do give their couples one or more books on marriage, such as the couple's workbook in this set, which has a chapter on sex. In addition, you may want to make available a book on sex (see Bibliography).

A majority of the pastors in our church refer a couple to an agency or another professional person for additional guidance in connection with their premarital preparation. Most of these referrals are to a family service or other counseling agency, or to a medical doctor. It is likely that much of this counseling is related to sexual adjustment (see chap. 7).

A growing number of ministers do give specific guidance in sexual adjustment. You can help educate couples by emphasizing, for example, the value of having a medical doctor give a full medical examination and advice on birth control, the importance of clitoral stimulation, or suggestions for easing the tension some couples may experience in intercourse.

You may do this in response to the couple's request for information on the premarital questionnaire in the couple's manual, especially question 34, or because of the implications of their answers to questions 30 through 35. When an individual indicates a need for it, some pastors administer the Sex Knowledge Inventory (see pp. 88-89).

Deciding just how much help to offer a couple grows out of what you discover about their strengths and weaknesses. These are the focus of the next chapter.

Chapter 7

Strengths and Weaknesses

Premarital preparation, especially in the premarital counseling sessions, is an effort to help a couple discover their strengths and weaknesses and to determine what additional guidance and resources they need in preparing for marriage.

For the couple, such discovery can be a means of identifying growth potential and enriching their relationship. It may also help them to discover areas of need and to assess their resources for meeting these needs.

For you, this is an opportunity to direct one or both of the partners to whatever additional resources may be needed. This process of discovery also guides you in deciding when it is wise to give sound reassurance or other forms of support and encouragement. You do not overlook problems. But the emphasis is on what can be done to solve them and on facilitating growth and change.[1]

Much of the preceding discussion related to self-understanding and adjustment may seem unduly slanted in the direction of individual problems or difficulties in adjustment between the partners. This is intentional, because the points at which there is a lack of understanding, an unrealistic expectation, or a problem of adjustment, are precisely the points where you may be most helpful to some couples. For other couples, however, a more positive kind of preparation may be appropriate. The emphasis in the following pages is on helping the couple discover and capitalize on their strengths.

Discovering Needs

First, we will give some attention to needs that have not yet been mentioned, or which have been referred to only briefly. We urge you to be alert to any physical, emotional, or intellectual difficulties that might overburden the marriage. Does either partner have any physical handicaps or limitations? Are both in good health? The answer to this last question, of course, is provided by a general health examination by a medical doctor.

Premarital Medical Examination

It is strongly recommended that, whenever possible, you insist that all couples see a physician, preferably one experienced in premarital counseling.[2] Most states require some kind of health examination in preparation for marriage, in addition to the traditional blood test. But many of these examinations are inadequate, and most of them cover much less than is recommended here. Such a premarital consultation with a medical doctor should include a general health examination, examination and consultation for sexual adjustment, and contraceptive information and prescription.

The first purpose of the premarital medical examination is to evaluate the general health and genetic history of both the man and the woman. This examination usually is related to their physical fitness for parenthood as well. This may not seem very important at the time of marriage, especially when a couple plans not to have children or to wait two or three years before having their first child.

We knew one such couple who found themselves with an unplanned pregnancy soon after marriage. The wife died in labor on her first wedding anniversary. The medical doctors who were called in said death was due partly to the fact that the baby was deformed and stillborn, and partly to lack of adequate medical care earlier. This recommendation for a premarital examination is not made out of fear that many couples will suffer a similar tragedy. (One is too many!) It is made out of the knowledge that couples need the information, guidance, and assurance that only a medical doctor can give.

The second purpose of the premarital medical examination is to check on the couple's readiness for sexual relations. If they are having intercourse already, as many couples are today, they may need help in improving their relationship. This is important for both the man and the woman. The couple may have questions and anxieties that call for the physician's guidance in helping them understand their sexual needs, and in overcoming the myth of naturalism.

A part of the woman's vaginal examination will be an examination of the hymen, to find out if it needs dilating in preparation for intercourse. Most women need no medical aid. But if dilation is indicated, it is usually accomplished artificially rather easily, or it may require a simple surgical procedure. Ordinarily this can be done in the physician's office with only a local anesthetic. Some women today still insist that defloration be done only by the husband in intercourse. A medical examination will indicate whether such a procedure is safe. Sometimes the hymen is so tough that entering marriage without medical help is risking too much suffering and placing too great a strain on the marital relationship.

This proved to be the case with one couple who came to a church counseling center for help with their sexual adjustment. They had been married six years and had two children. But they had never had a satisfying sex relationship, and the wife had never had an orgasm. In trying to discover the origin of their difficulty the pastoral counselor learned that complete intercourse was not possible for the first two years of marriage. The tough membrane made it impossible to penetrate the hymen. It was only after the hymen was ruptured during the birth of their first child that the vaginal orifice was enlarged enough to permit normal intercourse.

The counselor wondered how the couple had been able to endure the nervous tension caused by this condition during their first two years of marriage. He discovered that, fortunately, their overall relationship was strong enough to tolerate the sexual frustration.

It seems strange that anyone would be hesitant to accept the medical aid that is readily available today. But some people still need your insistence that the medical examination be a routine part of premarital preparation.

A third reason for the premarital medical consultation is to obtain information about family planning and birth control. More and more communities are developing Planned Parenthood clinics to give this service under competent medical supervision. Following the direction of a medical doctor or a clinic is the safest and best way to do family planning.

Many couples want to wait for a few years after marriage before starting a family. In such cases, only medically approved methods of contraception should be used, and these only under a physician's supervision. Because of possible side effects, the Pill should be used only by women who are under their doctor's care.

Some couples will also want information about the RH factor, and still others may need help in facilitating conception at the desired time.

Physicians qualified to give this kind of help, however, are hard to find. One study found that only 37 percent of the physicians interviewed "routinely made suggestions to premarital patients about contraceptive methods, whereas 28 percent included contraceptive information only if it was specifically requested by the patient." The figures relate only to contraceptive advice, for even fewer physicians offer "counsel concerning sexual and marital adjustment." More than 55 percent of the doctors reported that "nothing in their medical school education had prepared them for helping patients with marital adjustments." Also, more than 66 percent "reported negatively in this respect about their internship and residency training."[3] Fortunately this situation is improving today.

It is obvious that not every physician is equipped to offer the kind of premarital consultation recommended here. Thus, it may do little good simply to tell a couple to see their family doctor. It may be necessary to give them the names of two or more physicians who are known for this kind of counseling. We suggest that you visit physicians in your community to find out just what their practice is regarding the premarital consultation, and to find ways you and the physicians can work together for the good of the couple.

If no qualified physician is available in the immediate community, perhaps you can find one within a reasonable driving distance to whom you can refer them. Some couples may complain about such distances, but most of them drive farther than that to a football or basketball game!

Also, in most cities you will find marriage and sex therapists who are qualified to help couples with sexual and marital adjustment. We recommend that you check the Yellow Pages for persons who are certified by the American Association for Marriage and Family Therapy or the American Association of Sex Educators, Counselors and Therapists.[4]

Other Referrals

Are there any intellectual or emotional difficulties that might overburden the marriage? Does the premarital interview raise enough questions in your mind to indicate that intelligence or psychological testing is needed? If so, these tests require the services of a trained psychologist. Although giving some of the paper-and-pencil tests may be simple enough, interpreting them is another matter.

In most cases it will be best to delay further marriage preparation until any necessary testing and interpretation are completed. Even then, it may be necessary to refer some persons to a psychotherapist, to a social work agency, or to a mental health clinic where a psychiatric consultant is available. Again, we encourage you to know all such resources available in your community, or nearby, so as to make direct referrals when the need is indicated.

Referral is a delicate matter. It should be handled in a sensitive manner so that the person realizes that you do it out of genuine caring. Referral is a procedure which the couple must come to see as having real value for them—value enough for them to accept it positively and make good use of it.

Referrals may be needed in a variety of other areas, such as legal, financial, and household management. Legal questions may be as simple as asking about the requirements for obtaining a marriage license, which every pastor should know. Or questions may be more complicated, such as those related to property and alimony involvements carried over from a previous marriage, or grown children trying to prevent their aged father from changing his will in anticipation of a new marriage. Obviously it is unwise for you to do any guesswork here. Instead, you should be prepared to refer when necessary.

You may be able to help a couple set up a budget and to advise them regarding a joint checking account, but you may find it best to have a concerned banker or home economist to do this part of the marriage preparation regularly. At times some couples may also need the services of a loan officer or someone who can help them do some long-range planning in refinancing their school (or other) debts in order to be able to get married. Some couples may have money available for investment and need expert advice.

Others may need the guidance of the county welfare department, especially where grants to families of dependent children are being made for children from a former alliance, whether from legal or common-law marriage, or from no marriage at all. If a man or woman needs retraining for a new job before he or she can afford to get married, help may be available from the state vocational rehabilitation office.

For help in household management, the service of a home economist may be of great value. Many family service agencies offer this kind of help along with other kinds of counseling, including a rather full plan of premarital interviews. Counseling is usually a part of the service of Planned Parenthood clinics also.

Services available are so many and so varied that you need to know which are available in your community and to make good use of them. Most state mental health agencies (or similar groups) have directories of such services, free or for sale at very small cost.

Reading

In checking a couple's strong and weak points in marriage preparation, you are likely to find that most of them could benefit from more reading and study, either separately or together. In addition to the couple's workbook, which is strongly recommended as a gift to each couple at the very beginning of marriage preparation, most couples will need to do some other reading. For recommended readings, see the couple's workbook.

Mixed Marriages

Some couples will need help on special concerns, such as mixed marriages.[5] Mixed marriages, including interfaith marriages, are increasing.

In many communities Protestant-Catholic unions are the most numerous. We caution you not to operate out of outdated information, but to be aware that attitudes are changing. For example, the Roman Catholic Church has developed a "Theory Paper" based on Pope Paul VI's *Apostolic Letter Determining Norms for Mixed Marriage* (March, 1970). The emphasis is still on encouraging persons to marry within the Roman Catholic Church, but there is the recognition that many will not. For the latter there is the "pastoral" approach, which seeks to enhance the couple relationship and to encourage cooperation between the clergy of both of the partners so that the best pastoral care possible may be offered to the couple.

You may wish to contact the Catholic Diocese nearest you to ask for this and other educational materials which they provide for premarital preparation.

You may need to guide the couple in exploring their motivations for marriage, especially when a mixed marriage is being considered. This will require more time than is allowed in the four or five interviews suggested as the basic minimum in this manual.

In many, perhaps most, mixed marriages a couple may be drawn together by genuine love and a sense of basic similarity in values and interests which transcends their differences and is truly much more important to them. Such couples need your help in realistically facing tensions their differences may create within marriage as well as any difficulties with others outside their marriage. But they also deserve your support in facing necessary adjustments, and your reassurance when you discover their strengths.

Some other couples, however, may be driven to marriage by rebellion against their parent(s) or against social pressures to "marry your own kind." This rebellion may be a deeply neurotic desire to punish their parents. Some marry outside their ethnic group because they feel rejected by their own group. Others may marry out of a desire to accelerate social reform, as is believed to be the case in some interracial and interethnic marriages today. Still others marry out of a sense of adventure, in response to the glamor of the mysterious in a person from a different origin or background. Some intercultural marriages occur simply because of the proximity of two people at the age of marriage.

Another reason for some mixed marriages is the expectation of personal, social, or economic gain as, for example, when one "marries up" for personal gain of one kind or another. Or a man who does not like the present egalitarian relationship between men and women gaining support in the United States today may seek marriage with a woman from another culture who has been trained to look up to men. She may make him feel superior.

You may sometimes discover that motivations for marriage seem to be unsound. Then you may feel that you must recommend that the couple postpone their wedding, perhaps to allow for additional counseling. If they are unwilling to postpone you may decide to go ahead and marry them.

On occasion, after you have helped a couple to question the soundness of their motivations, they may postpone their marriage, and later may break off their relationship altogether. Their motives, what-ever they may be, should be explored so that they may be understood, and perhaps changed, or strengthened. In any case, the couple will then be able to make their decision on the basis of deeper understanding. And again, it is their decision.

Discovering Strengths

As you help couples discover the strengths and weaknesses they bring to marriage, you may be surprised to find that they have more strengths than weaknesses. The reason for your surprise is understandable. So much pastoral counseling is problem-centered: persons with problems they cannot handle alone come to you for help. We urge you not to become so absorbed in the problem-centered approach that even in premarital preparation you see only the difficulties.

Preoccupation with problems poses real dangers. One is the possibility of giving couples the negative impression that you are always looking for problems and are unable to see their strong points. This may cause them to resist your help or to misuse it. Premarital preparation must deal with any problems that need attention, of course. But it must also help couples develop their strong points, strengthen and improve some of the positive growing edges of their relationship.

To the extent that it is really appropriate, marriage preparation should put emphasis on the strengths of the couple. We hope you will call attention to, and explore, their strengths in a positive, affirming manner. We believe the growth potential is within each person and each couple you work with. Furthermore, we believe that through experiencing your pastoral care and guidance these persons may "actualize" their potential.

Being alert to the strengths a couple bring to marriage, you may be impressed by three qualities that are often overlooked—their desire for preparation, their potential for growth and change, and their determination to succeed in marriage.

Many couples will be open to receiving all the help they can get, not because they approach marriage with a great deal of fear or uncertainty, or are overloaded with problems, but because they realize that marriage is an important and sometimes difficult undertaking. They have been educated through the ministry of the church—through the ongoing curriculum of the church school, through special series of seminars, through personal experiences with married couples (hopefully including their parents), and of course, through your sermons! And they know from their friends and family that a satisfying marriage does not just happen, but requires a commitment to work. So they appreciate all the help you can give them. This may sound strange since so many pastors are still struggling with the problem of getting couples to contact them for premarital preparation. Yet this appreciative attitude is being expressed by more and more couples today, as they discover the value of preparing for marriage.

A couple does not have to be perfect to insure a sound marriage. If that were so, there never would be any satisfying marriages! Accepting the fact that we are all imperfect human beings has real value. It keeps us from expecting too much of ourselves and permits us to be more understanding of our partners.

But this is not the kind of acceptance that means passive resignation. In a very real sense this is accepting one's shortcomings as *a challenge to change and to improve.* As we have said, most persons are endowed with an ability to grow and to change for the better. They have a God-given inner drive toward wholeness that responds to intelligent direction. This potential for growth is one of the greatest strengths a couple brings to marriage.

Many authorities feel that *a couple's greatest strength is the determination to make their marriage work,* or the drive to succeed. It is an unwillingness to give up, or to consider divorce as an easy way out.

You may find that this determination greatly increases a couple's ability to utilize marriage counseling as a resource. Two persons are determined to do their best to get the most out of their marriage. And this is one of the powerful forces for enrichment in marriage, and needs to be supported and encouraged.

What are some other strengths to be alert to? What should be encouraged? At what point is reassurance warranted?

In trying to answer these questions, it is essential not to gloss over problems. It is critical not to give false reassurance in the face of a difficult problem: "Oh, don't worry about that; you won't have any trouble working that out when it comes along"—particularly when there is no basis for such a statement. Instead, we hope you will be sensitive to basic strong points that can be built upon, that can serve as the foundation for new growth and greater strength. Begin with reality and build upon it.

Many couples coming to you to be married will show an adequate understanding of the nature of marriage. Perhaps they have carefully evaluated their love to be sure it is true love, and they plan to be faithful to each other. Many of them will not be rushing into marriage blindly, but rather have been very careful in making the decisions regarding their engagement of several months and in setting the date for the wedding. Some of them will be very serious about their marriage as a sacred commitment to each other in a lifelong covenant relationship.

As a sensitive pastor you can pick up such important understandings and try *to help enlarge their meanings for the couple.* For example, you might explore with the couple ways in which they may enrich their understanding of love and fidelity, and help them appreciate some dimensions they may not have been aware of before. One example is enlarging the meaning of fidelity to include much more than faithfulness in sex relations. Here is an opportunity for you as a spiritual guide to help couples consider the theological implications of what true faithfulness means. For us faithfulness is recognizing the sacred worth of one's partner and being dedicated to the partner's welfare, as well as one's own, hence working toward an egalitarian relationship.

You may work with a couple to help them discover other areas for growth, rooted in their already sound understandings. Both persons may be dedicated Christians, and may be actively related to the church. Through free question-and-answer discussion, they may come to see more clearly the value of Christian character in marriage. They may give some evidence of being able to give and receive love, but questioning may reveal that they need to give more attention to the forgiving aspects of love.

Discussion may bring out the fact that they are actually searching for guidance in readjusting as a married pair to some of the fellowship and service activities they have been related to previously. They may be afraid of being cut off from old groups, and uncertain about new ones open to them. They may want their life together to be based on concern for others as they express it through their work—she as a nurse and he as a teacher, for example. Perhaps after sharing some of the positive values and meanings of their work, a couple may be ready for some exploration of how their concern for others can reach beyond the persons they serve directly.

The above is not meant to suggest that you manipulate couples into preconceived patterns. Rather, it is intended as an example of how recognized strong points may serve as the basis for further discussion that may result in deeper enrichment or wider horizons.

It may be easy for you to respond with deep feeling for a person who is struggling with a problem, for you are aware of the person's need for your concern and support in working it through. It may be more difficult, however, to respond to a fairly mature person, because it may seem that that person does not need you. We believe that the fullest enrichment and growth of a mature person may also be stimulated by your expression of genuine encouragement and by your openness to accept and assist them in growing.

In your premarital preparation, we believe you are justified in giving support and encouragement to a person entering marriage *when the person demonstrates an understanding of self.* This may be evident when the person knows who he or she is and shows mature judgment and intelligence in practical affairs. You may see it in a healthy affirmation of sexuality, although there may be a need for some fuller understanding of sexual relations. Self-understanding may be reflected when a person understands fairly well what he or she brings to marriage in terms of philosophy and a system of values, various aspects of his or her background, personal characteristics, interests, and activities. You may feel good about supporting a person who is reasonably healthy emotionally.

In summary, we recommend again the judicious use of reassurance and support to stimulate further growth, both for the individuals and for their relationship. Many couples will be fairly realistic about the adjustments they will be making in marriage. They may have reasonably high expectations of each other and of marriage that are in line with their abilities. Neither person expects the other to be perfect. Instead, they accept their immaturities, but have a healthy desire to change, to grow, and to improve. They know they will have to work at their marriage. They are aware of certain differences, tensions, and conflicts, and are realistic in expecting

some of these to continue after marriage. They already have some experience in working through conflict in several areas. They give evidence of communicating with each other in some depth. They indicate some skill in problem-solving.

Many couples will realize that they are adjusting to marriage as well as to each other. Their personalities may be complementary and compatible. They may enjoy many common interests and activities, but also grant each other the freedom to be separate individuals.

Even before they come for marriage preparation, many couples will have evaluated specific areas of their adjustment, such as religion, sex, money, and their relationship with relatives. They may be active in a church, though perhaps not in the same church. Their income may be adequate, and they may be planning a sensible budget and household-management procedures. They may express warm feelings for each other, as well as negative ones, and have healthy attitudes regarding sex. Some couples will give indications that they are being sensible about preparing for most of the developmental tasks they will face all through marriage. Most couples will also have strong positive feelings about their marriage and will be entering it with a feeling of confidence and a sense of "belonging to each other" in the best sense of that phrase.

All in all, you may have a very good feeling about a couple's readiness for marriage. If you do, there is no reason why you should not share your feeling with the couple. This kind of genuine reassurance may relieve some of the tension they are bound to feel and stimulate them to grow in their relationship. A growing relationship calls for productive communication and problem-solving—which is the concern of the next chapter.

One of the major purposes in marriage preparation is to facilitate and improve communication between the partners. We believe communication is the key to a deep and intimate relationship. Unfortunately, far too few people have the skills to communicate effectively, though more training is being offered today through churches, schools, businesses, and community organizations.[1]

Because it is still difficult for many to communicate effectively, we think one of your important tasks will be to take the couple through some of the exercises in their workbook, chapter 4 (we think it is a good idea for you to try these with your spouse, or with a trusted friend if you are single). You may then help them practice listening and understanding in their dynamic interaction.

This means that your premarital sessions either begin or improve the process of deeper sharing that is expected to continue and grow in marriage. You also can help the couple discover the value of problem-solving and increase their decision-making skills. You may do this by actually applying these skills to specific areas of their relationship when there is conflict or an issue to be resolved.

An Interactive Process

Communication is the dynamic interaction of two (or more) persons involving some kind of message and response, usually conveying both feelings and ideas, which may be expressed in actions as well as words.

We believe there are four elements in genuine communication that need to be emphasized: (1) sending and responding, (2) ideas and feelings, (3) words and actions, and (4) openness and respect for privacy.

Sending and Responding

In marriage preparation you may help a couple understand and experience the fact that communication is a two-way process. It is not a matter of one person "telling" the other something, to which he or she pays almost no attention. Unless someone is listening—really listening and responding to what is being said—the message is not getting through. Of course, the response may occur in silence. It does not have to be expressed orally. It may be happening in the mind of the listener. But this is a response. Communication, then, is not monologue, but dialogue. Both a sender and a responder are necessary.

Much of the time, however, one person does not hear what is actually said. One hears only one's own interpretation of the message. Is it any wonder, then, that the message that gets through is so often very different from the one that is intended? It is important that the responder try to understand what the message means to the sender. It is also essential for the sender to try to send clear signals.

In all communication, but especially in communication in marriage, it is essential for the responder, not only to get the message, but to respond appropriately. For couples, this means being sensitive to each other's needs and responding appropriately to those needs. If one is either unwilling or unable to "hear" the other's needs or to make a response to them, the relationship will suffer.

Your own modeling can be very helpful to the couple. The way you interact with them, their feeling understood by you, your *being there* for them—these can be opportunities for them to learn and to improve their communication.

We suggest that you take time now to invite someone close to you (your spouse if you are married) to practice

*sending and responding to a message with you. Use the
end of chapter 4 in the couple's manual to rate yourselves
on both segments.*

Persons can learn to be more sensitive listeners
and to respond more appropriately. They can also
learn to communicate better. Premarital preparation
offers an opportunity for such learning.

Ideas and Feelings

The message in communication usually conveys
ideas and feelings, and both are important. But
frequently the intellectual concept is emphasized,
while the emotional content is almost completely
overlooked or ignored. Many couples make the
mistake of trying to interact with each other on the
rational level and forgetting or overlooking the
feelings.

To illustrate: A young wife came home from work
and complained to her husband, "The boss really
messed things up for me at the office today. You
remember he let me handle the correspondence on
that Randall account? Well, today, without saying a
word to me about it, he just dictated another letter
changing the specifications I sent to them yester-
day."

To which the husband replied, "Well, he's the
boss. That's his job." And then he wondered why
she stormed out with "Oh, men!"

What the husband said was true. He stated a fact,
on the rational level. But he missed the emotional
meaning of what his wife had said. If he had been
more receptive of the feeling in what she said, he
might have replied, "Yeah, it's pretty tough being
pushed aside and contradicted." On receiving this
kind of sensitive response, instead of storming out,
she might have been able to experience a sense of
release from the tension she had been carrying all
day. Probably she would have a feeling of warmth for
a husband who understood! And probably, too, she
would be able to discover her own ability to deal with
the problem objectively.

You can assist couples in being more sensitive to
each other's feelings. You can guide them in finding
ways of helping each other express their true
feelings. You can help them see that both their
positive and negative feelings need to be brought out
into the open so they can be understood and handled
constructively by the two of them. You can point out
the danger in hiding feelings, because you know
that, hidden, they are likely to cause additional hurt;
suppressed, they are likely to fester and worsen.

They may cause the individual more inner uneasi-
ness and may also damage the relationship with the
partner, perhaps without either one realizing what is
causing the trouble. These unacknowledged feelings
do not just go away!

Words and Actions

Communication can take the form of actions as
well as words. Some couples make the mistake of
thinking that they are communicating only when
they are talking to each other. To be sure, words are
important, but behavior—gestures, facial expressions, mannerisms, posture, and even silence, as
well as specific acts—may convey much more than
words, or at least with more force. A slammed door,
for example, may communicate anger more effectively than words do.

You can help a couple see that behavior is a form of
communication, and can help them learn how to
interpret the meaning of their behavior. You can also
help couples see that there is danger in playing down
the importance of words. They need to know that it is
essential for them to take time to talk things over. If
they keep on saying "Not now, we'll talk about that
later," they may find so much unfinished business
piling up that they are never quite able to catch up.
And their relationship may suffer.

Why is communication so important? Real communication is not simply what happens *between* a
couple, as though the process were something
external, something suspended between them.
Rather, it is the dynamic involvement of two persons
in each other's lives. This kind of communication is a
necessity in marriage if there is to be an in-depth
relationship.

Some kind of communication is essential to the
psychic health and growth of the individual. The
maintenance of life depends on one's being able to
communicate the message of one's own selfhood to
another and being able to receive a similar message
from another in response. Emotional starvation can
result if a person does not receive this kind of
communication. Without the ability to communicate,
an individual would become completely isolated
from others, and his or her very personhood would
atrophy.

Free and spontaneous communication is also
essential to the development of an intimate relationship between two people. Thus they share each
other's lives. A genuine sense of belonging develops
between them. They feel secure with each other and
have a sense of comfort and stability in their

relationship. A deep and open communication between a man and a woman makes possible the enrichment of their relationship through a sharing of their sufferings and struggles, their values and aspirations.

Developing open communication through marriage preparation is especially important, because couples usually have some negative conditioning to overcome. Modest progress certainly can be made with some, but the barriers to open communication are often high, and extensive help may be necessary.

Most persons have been trained not to express certain feelings or interests. They learn to hide behind masks, so that it is very difficult for one person to get to know another. Perhaps because of unpleasant, or even traumatic, experiences, many learn to protect themselves from the possibility of being hurt again. Hence they close down certain lines of communication.

Even in marriage some couples find that they are constantly hurting each other because they are not fully or accurately communicating. So they close off one area after another, supposedly out of positive consideration for each other, until there is very little open relationship left to them. Some authorities believe that lack of communication is the chief source of difficulty in 85 percent of the unhappy marriages.

In premarital preparation you can help couples see the importance of communication in their developing relationship, for marriage at its best is an intimate relationship and must be nourished to grow. Genuine communication is one way to nourish a relationship. Since marriage is a dynamic, ever-changing relationship, there must be continuing interaction between the partners. Without communication, two people would remain two private, isolated individuals. Marriage is an achievement that requires the cooperation of both husband and wife. Inevitably, tensions and disagreements will arise in the normal course of living. These can be faced and worked out together—through communication.

Having emphasized openness, we now want to stress the individual's right to *privacy*. So much is being said today about sharing everything one thinks or feels, that there is almost a demand to "tell all." We believe it is important for a mate to invite the partner to share, but we also believe it is the partner's responsibility to decide whether to share or not to share. Helping a couple to appreciate this dimension of communication can help them feel respected by each other. And this, we think, will result in more openness in their communication.

In summary, we are saying that effective couple communication has four elements that need to be emphasized: (1) It is an interactive process between the two persons. (2) It involves ideas and feelings. (3) It includes words and actions. (4) It requires openness as well as respect for privacy. Now let us look at some of the ways in which you can help with this process.

There is some value in helping the couple discover some of the barriers to communication with each other. They may discover that they are too busy to talk things over, much as they need to or want to. This may be especially true of a couple in the rush of the last few days before the wedding.

One person may complain that the other does not listen when he or she is talking, or does not take seriously what he or she says. The other may respond negatively to small talk and retreat from communication because nothing important seems to be happening. Being all wrapped up in personal interests and concerns can also block communication. This preoccupation can vary from a temporary concentration on one's own affairs to a thorough-going self-centeredness.

Even though one must express real feelings to communicate in depth, emotions can also block communication. These emotions can be guilt feelings, feelings of inferiority, of hostility or resentment, or of simple fatigue. The couple may be helped to see, for example, that there are times when it is best to postpone working on a problem until they can work on it more constructively.

It might be helpful, also, for you to guide the couple in evaluating ways of overcoming any barriers to communication that they discover in their relationship. They may come to realize that real communication does take time and effort, and cannot be achieved on the run. They may have to plan their schedule so it allows them more time together. They may discover that it is necessary to make a continuing effort to listen, to try hard to "be there 100 percent" instead of wandering off on their own concerns. This may suggest that one partner will need to become more interested in the activities and concerns of the other. Of course this does not mean that only one person does all the listening. We are suggesting that the partners need to take turns listening and responding to "be there 100 percent"!

Some couples may discover that one or both of them have some deep negative feelings that they need to work through with you or another counselor. They may find that any improvement in communication lies in an individual's becoming the kind of person who is easy to talk with. Others may find that they need more sharing of values and interests so as to develop more common goals and activities. Still other couples may discover that one or both partners need more freedom to develop personal interests in order to have something significant to share when they do have time together.

Counseling Stimulates Communication

Perhaps the best way to stimulate communication between two persons is to let it happen naturally in the process of premarital preparation.

The very fact that the couple has agreed to come to you may start them talking about the seriousness of their marriage. Or communication may be stimulated by one of them (usually the woman) accepting the pastor's invitation to the first interview, even though the other is questioning the value of such help. She, for example, may have to do quite a bit of communicating to get her fiancé to agree to come in, and they may discuss a number of concerns that are pretty important to her in the process. This may happen entirely outside the sessions.

In the sessions themselves, some issues or concerns may be brought out into the open, which the couple may have been avoiding in an effort to keep down conflict. They may begin to talk over some of these with you, but continue their conversations on their own. You may sense an area of need and open it up for this purpose. Or there may be some topics they have already talked about, but only superficially, and then pushed aside, thinking they had covered the subject. You can encourage them to pursue these in greater depth simply by asking a few questions that have some meaning for them (but of course, not probing!).

When you read the wedding ritual to a couple, and they begin to discuss certain points, communication may be initiated that will continue long after the session is over. During the joint interview, one partner may notice the other's reaction to a particular statement or question. He or she may not say anything about it at the time, but later may inquire about its meaning, and a whole flow of conversation may follow.

In addition, *you have an opportunity for stimulating greater communication in the private appointment(s)*. For example, there may be an issue that should be faced by the couple, but for one reason or another, they hesitate to get into it. In the confidentiality of the private appointment one partner may muster enough courage to bring it up.

This is exactly what happened in one session with a man alone. The pastor, reflecting on the young man's feeling that he did not expect to have any "trouble" after marriage, went on to ask, "If you could imagine yourself having some disagreement after marriage, what do you think it might be about?"

The young man hesitated for a long time, obviously searching. Finally he answered, "It might be over her father. I think she feels too close to him."

So they took time to explore the meaning of these feelings for the new relationship. This particular young man gained enough strength in the private interview to discuss the father-daughter relationship with his partner, and discovered that it was not as much of a problem as he had feared. He later shared with his pastor his conclusion that, without the stimulus of the question, he might never have brought his fear out into the open and discussed it, and might have been overly sensitive about it for years to come.

This is the kind of fear that one person might hesitate to bring up with the partner present. Most engaged persons are afraid to express any concern about the other's family, especially the parents, and especially not within a few weeks of the wedding! Thus the private appointment can stimulate conversation, not only between the individual and you, but also between the partners.

One of the most effective ways of stimulating communication is through the *use of the premarital questionnaires* in the back of the couple's workbook (see detailed instructions for use of the questionnaires, beginning on p. 83). Each person filling out the questionnaire will probably find questions about many items he or she had not previously considered important. Now the person begins to wonder, "If these are important enough to be on the form, I guess they are important enough for us to discuss." Thus, couples may begin to talk about new subjects.

Or partners, as each fills out his or her own questionnaire, may become curious about what kind of answer the other gave to a particular question. One may ask, "How did you answer number 30 about affection?" and "Can you tell me more?" Thus, a new line of communication is initiated.

Even though you instruct each person to fill out the questionnaire alone, you may tell couples that as soon as they have completed the form they may talk about any of the questions. In fact, it will be helpful to encourage them to do so.

Communication may also be stimulated by the way you use the questionnaires. In comparing the man's answers with those of the woman, you may discover some significant differences. In the private appointment, and without violating the confidence of either person, you can explore reasons for their answers.

The reading you ask the couple to do may also initiate deeper communication. From our experience, the woman usually takes more time for reading. Frequently she may share with her partner some of the information she has gained.

You might ask a couple to read a book together. Or you might suggest that they read certain chapters on particular subjects, thus encouraging extended conversation on particular topics. You could bring some of the reading into the conversation during the interviews and suggest further homework for the couple. A few couples take time to read portions of one or more books aloud and then talk about them. Reading aloud together a devotional book such as Ross Synder's *Inscape* or David Mace's *Whom God Hath Joined* may encourage a couple to have further conversation about some very significant areas of their relationship in the light of their Christian faith.

Problem-Solving

A crucial dimension of communication is decision-making and problem-solving. Here you, the pastor, have the opportunity to deal with conflict in the context of the Christian faith. How does the *covenant relationship* make a difference in working through disagreements?

What is your own experience with your spouse or a significant person in your life? We suggest that the two of you go through the material in the couple's manual, chapter 5. What new insights do you have regarding your own creative use of conflict?

In the sessions, you can help couples develop the ability to make decisions together and solve problems as they come along. Think about how your own personal experience and attitude can contribute to the process. You can encourage a couple to take an optimistic attitude toward their marriage, so that they expect the best from each other without expecting too much. At the same time, you can help them to be realistic in anticipating disagreements and to be prepared to cope with disagreements as they arise. Expecting some differences will help a couple resist panic when they have their first quarrel. They will not feel that their marriage is destroyed by one argument. You can also emphasize that conflict, when handled properly, can become a powerful motivation for improving their marriage. And it can

also bring the couple closer as they experience the true meaning of reconciliation (and forgiveness, if there has been hurt).

By constructively facing any conflict that arises during the session, you can help a couple experience the benefits of such an encounter.

Take, as an example, John and Sally. In the middle of their second joint interview with their pastor, John has just expressed a rather strong feeling about money. They will have to make some sacrifices until he "can get a better job," he says.

Sally volunteers, "We can always get money from my dad."

The pastor asks Sally how John feels about that. She seems surprised at the question, but says she does not know.

The pastor turns to John and asks, "How do you feel about that, John?"

He replies with deep emotion, "I wouldn't like it!" He raises his voice, "In fact, I wouldn't like it at all!"

Can you put yourself in that pastor's place? What would you do after this outburst? More important, how would you feel while it was happening? What effect do you think your feelings would have on Sally? On John? What would you do next? Would you do or say anything at this point?

Our experience is that people usually shy away from conflict. Perhaps in the past there have been deep hurts and damaged relationships. Your tendency may be, for example, to "reconcile" John and Sally prematurely. "Peace at any price" may be your feeling.

But we believe that such a couple in conflict calls for your support and your encouraging them to stay with the problem. At this point, you need not be concerned about the outcome. You are supporting them in the process of confronting an issue that needs to be explored at the feeling level. It is far more helpful, of course, for them to experience an accepting attitude from you.

In addition, it may be important for you to give some verbal reassurance to back up your attitude, and to clarify in their minds what you really mean. This kind of attitude and verbal assurance can help to head off any guilt feelings that might follow such an outburst and that might cause either person to withdraw. It can also clear the way for further exploration of the issue, and can aid in getting at the roots of the conflict. This means that you are not taking sides with, or blaming, one or both persons. Instead, you will be helping them focus on, and explore, the meaning of the issue that gave rise to the strong feelings.

This may be the beginning point for them in learning some of the steps to follow in solving their problem. We emphasize here your helping the couple with the *process* and leaving them responsible for finding their own solutions. We refer the couple to chapter 5 of their workbook for a model for working through conflict.

Basic Steps

We suggest five basic steps in problem-solving: (1) define the problem; (2) gather data; (3) explore alternatives; (4) choose one alternative and act on it; and (5) assess the results.[2]

When related to marriage problems, Steps Three and Four as listed above had best be expanded, as will be explained. Normally these steps are followed in order, but not necessarily. For example, a couple may discover that the process of gathering data about the causes of a conflict creates enough understanding to make going through the other steps unnecessary. On the other hand, in the process of exploring alternatives, they may discover another, more urgent, problem and decide to double back immediately to Step One to work on it.

Here are these basic steps in problem-solving, briefly described, as they may be followed in the session or by the couple on their own:

1. *Define the problem.* Deciding what the problem is may be much more difficult than it seems at first. Maybe that is why some people say that "defining the problem is half the solution." Many couples will find it hard to admit that they have a problem. They may need help in facing it squarely for what it is. Together a couple should try to put into words just what the problem is so they can agree on what it is they are working on. If it is not a "mutually defined" problem, they may be moving in opposite directions. One of your major tasks in this kind of situation is to help the couple focus on the problem and attack it instead of each other. Here again you may need to remind them of the covenant relationship, and their commitment to each other's welfare should be renewed.

While you are helping a couple define a problem, several related issues may emerge. Then you can help facilitate their sorting through these issues and focusing on one problem.

An important part of defining the problem is having each state how the problem affects him or her. How does the problem make *him* feel? How does it make *her* feel? This is hard for many, especially for those who are unaccustomed to sharing feelings. We believe that stating the problem in rational terms is only half-defining the issue; both the rational and the emotional elements are important.

2. *Gather data.* Next, they need to get all the pertinent information about the problem that is necessary. They should list all the possible causes they can think of. This can be a very painful process for some. Together they should try to figure out what led up to the problem, and what brings it to a head just now. Generally, the more detailed they can be about the origin and development of the problem, the better they will be able to understand it.

Again, you may help the couple direct their energies to the causes of the problem rather than blame each other. You can also help them to be sure that they are getting at the roots of their problem and digging them out, instead of only chopping off the problem at the surface and leaving the roots to produce more problems in the future.

3. *Explore alternatives.* This step is a whole process in itself. Before actually listing the various alternatives for action, the couple should set some goals. The emphasis should now be placed on the positive side. What is it they want to accomplish together? You may need to encourage them to do some dreaming about what they would like to have in their marriage in the place of the difficulty that has arisen. You should also check to be sure they are being realistic about the possibilities they consider. Are they choosing their purposes together? For if one does all the choosing, and the other only tags along, neither will have very strong motivation for working toward a solution. And the "tag along" most likely will build resentment and hostility.

Next, you may aid the couple in listing all possible alternatives and in gathering all the information and insights available regarding each solution. Do they need to do some reading? Do they need information or guidance from experienced people or professionals?

You may guide each person in trying to put himself or herself in the other's place. Each needs to try to find out how the other really feels about the problem and its possible solutions. Is there anything holding them back from expressing their opinions or sharing their real feelings? How can you help both of the partners to express themselves freely and frankly?

Then you may assist the couple in actually listing all possible alternatives. What can the couple do about the problem to move toward a solution? What can the partners do separately? What can they do together? How does each person feel about each of the alternatives? Which alternatives promise some real help? Is the couple moving toward the goals agreed upon?

4. *Choose one alternative and act on it.* This is the point at which you can help a couple evaluate each of the possible alternatives in order to narrow down the list to one course of action. To do this, make sure the couple examine the positive and negative aspects of each alternative. What does each alternative have going for it? What forces might block it? How does each measure up in terms of its values? At this point be sure the couple check each alternative against their goals to make certain it has a good chance of accomplishing the purpose desired.

Now the couple are ready to decide which seems to be the best course of action. They will need to determine exactly what is to be done. Who does what? Do they need help from others? While you may support them in the decision and the action, the couple need to put their plan into practice. They should try it out.

5. *Assess the results.* Actually, evaluation should take place at every step in the process as the partners ask each other, How are you doing? You will be asking yourself: What is happening to them—these persons—in the process? What is happening to their relationship? Are they becoming more mature persons in the process? Will what they are learning from working through their problem help them in the future?

You may also have additional questions. If the problem is not solved or the issue is not resolved, is it wise for the couple to repeat the problem-solving process? Or is this a condition or situation they must continue to live with without an immediate solution? Is the solution learning to cope with the status quo? How much more can they do on their own, or do they need additional professional help to discover new insights about themselves or their situation before moving farther in problem-solving?

Finally, you may need to help couples evaluate their effectiveness in problem-solving on their own, and *recognize when they need to seek outside, perhaps professional, help.* Here are some simple guidelines.

Couples need help (1) when they are unable to agree that a problem exists, yet one is very upset about it while the other is not concerned; (2) when they both agree they "have a problem" but are unable to define it; (3) when they try to go through the steps of problem-solving but never seem to get anywhere; (4) whenever communication breaks down and they simply cannot talk about the problem (a clear signal to call in help!); (5) if their efforts to improve their relationship only make matters worse.

Throughout the process of preparing for marriage you are building a pastoral relationship with the couple(s). How to develop the pastoral relationship is the concern of the next chapter.

The last major purpose of premarital preparation is to establish or strengthen a pastoral relationship with the couple. Although placed last, this is one of the most important purposes of marital preparation. Establishing a strong pastoral relationship is important for the couple, especially if they should need to return for marriage counseling.

What is meant here is much broader than the counseling relationship itself, although this is part of it. We are thinking of a pastoral relationship that extends far beyond the premarital sessions. For some couples, this relationship may have been established before these sessions. If so, premarital preparation should deepen it. If there has been no deep relationship before, it may begin in group marriage preparation, and especially in premarital counseling.

Dynamic Interaction

This pastoral relationship is a dynamic interacting of two (or more) persons, in this case you, the pastor, and one person, or you and the couple, or you and a group of couples. In these interactions, the relationship grows out of the sharing of feelings and attitudes, the suffering and struggles, or the joys and aspirations of the engaged persons with you. It grows when you, their pastor, respect, accept, care about, and affirm them as persons of infinite worth.

In some respects this relationship is like a bridge joining two islands. Contrary to John Donne, each person is, in a very real sense, an island of private consciousness, which can be shared with another only as bridges of understanding are built between them.

The relationship may be initiated by either the pastor or the person. If an individual or a couple are aware of a problem that calls for counseling, they

may make the first contact by asking for help. Usually, however, the pastor initiates the relationship by asking the couple to come for the premarital sessions. Either one may reach out to the other, but for a relationship to be established the other must make a response. Without both the reaching-out and the responding there is no relating, no real meeting of persons.

To have any dependable stability, the relationship must be anchored deep within the being of each person. A superficial anchorage at either end makes for a flimsy relationship, which may break down at any time. The amount of traffic or weight it can carry depends on the strength, or quality, of the relationship.

What is it that gives quality to this relationship? As a pastor, what can you *be* and *do* that will inspire the kind of response that will aid personal growth and enrich the marriage of a couple? The suggestions that follow are not neatly categorized, but are perspectives on the helping relationship, whether that relationship be in group work or in counseling sessions. Each perspective is very much interrelated with all the others, for each is a facet of the whole relationship.

First, can you *love?* Love leads to trust. When you truly care about, and really want to help, the persons you work with, a genuine warmth and concern is communicated. Unless they have been so severely hurt in other relationships that they have been forced to "close up" in order to protect themselves, most persons are likely to respond positively, even though cautiously. They may move toward you slowly, checking out the relationship to see "what is in it for them." At first they may respond by testing more than by trusting. As they discover that your concern is genuine, that you really are dependable, they are likely to become more open and willing to share. In short, they may become more trusting and may really work at building a strong relationship.

Second, can you show *respect* for the persons you are working with? Respect encourages responsibility. When you show respect for an individual as a person, that individual may be freed to discover inner resources and to take more responsibility for himself or herself, or for the marriage relationship. We believe you will find that this is especially true when you express respect by trusting persons to make their own decisions, or by recognizing them as free agents who are responsible for themselves. In this way you help people stand on their own feet, rather than make them dependent on you. You allow them the freedom to fail.

This means that you will not attempt to do too much for those you are helping. You allow them to move at their own pace. It also means that you will not threaten them by probing. Instead, you respect their privacy, and go only as far as they are ready to move at the moment. You keep confidences, for you respect them as persons, and never see them as objects to be used for your purposes.

Can you accept them? *Acceptance* enhances understanding. When persons are accepted as they are, they may be encouraged to share more of their inner selves, and in the process may gain more insight into themselves. Or as the partners learn that their relationship is accepted for what it is, they may share more of their deeper feelings about it and so gain a better understanding of what it means to them. Instead of being rejected, the person, or the couple, and their relationship need to be accepted as they are.

In this accepting spirit, then, you may listen, not only to the words, but primarily to the heartbeat, and try to reflect the feelings that may be hidden between the words. If you are sensitive enough to reflect these feelings accurately, the person is likely to feel that you really understand.

A genuine desire on your part to understand, with repeated efforts to clarify, has almost the same positive effect as actually understanding. When persons feel accepted and understood, they can drop some of their defenses, which may have been consuming much of their energy. Then they can put that energy into learning to understand themselves and into improving their relationship.

Can you affirm persons who come to you? *Affirmation* stimulates growth. As helpful as acceptance is, we believe it does not go far enough. We believe you need to affirm each person as a child of God. This means that, instead of judging, condemning, or correcting an individual, you will make every effort to appreciate that person in the process of becoming, as one appreciates and enjoys a sunset unfolding its beauty. This positive affirmation of personhood sustains an individual in a supportive relationship when it is needed. This kind of affirmation helps give a person a sense of self-confidence, the genuine self-esteem so essential to the ability to love another. It also inspires and challenges a person to become his or her best possible self under God, and to give of himself or herself to another.

A Helping Relationship

The pastoral relationship is a helping relationship. Out of his rich experience in counseling, Carl Rogers suggests a series of ten questions you might ask yourself in seeking to create a helping relationship, both in premarital preparation and in your continuing pastoral care. You may want to ask yourself these questions using more inclusive language to relate to women as well as men.

1. Can I be in some way which will be perceived by the other person as trustworthy, as dependable or consistent in some deep sense? I used to feel that if I fulfilled all the outer conditions of trustworthiness—keeping appointments, respecting the confidential nature of the interviews, etc.—this condition would be fulfilled. But experience drove home the fact that to act consistently acceptant, for example, if in fact I was feeling annoyed or skeptical or some other non-acceptant feeling, was certain in the long run to be perceived as inconsistent or untrustworthy. I have come to recognize that being trustworthy does not demand that I be rigidly consistent but that I be dependably real. . . .

2. Can I be expressive enough as a person that what I am will be communicated unambiguously? When I am experiencing an attitude of annoyance toward another person but am unaware of it, then my communication contains contradictory messages. My words are giving one message, but I am also in subtle ways communicating the annoyance I feel and this confuses the other person and makes him distrustful, though he too may be unaware of what is causing the difficulty. . . .

3. Can I let myself experience positive attitudes toward this other person—attitudes of warmth, caring, liking, interest, respect? It is not easy. I find in myself, and feel that I often see in others, a certain amount of fear of these feelings. We are afraid that if we let ourselves freely experience these positive feelings toward another we may be trapped by them. They may lead to demands on us or we may be disappointed in our trust, and these outcomes we fear. So as a reaction we tend to build up distance between ourselves and others—aloofness, a "professional" attitude, an impersonal relationship. . . .

4. Can I be strong enough as a person to be separate from the other? Can I be a sturdy respecter of my own feelings, my own needs, as well as his? Can I own and, if need be, express my own feelings as something belonging to me and separate from his feelings? When I can freely feel this strength of being a separate person, then I find that I can let myself go much more deeply in understanding and accepting him because I am not fearful of losing myself. . . .

5. Am I secure enough within myself to permit him his separateness? Can I permit him to be what he is—honest or deceitful, infantile or adult, despairing or overconfident? Can I give him the freedom to be? Or do I feel that he should follow my advice, or remain somewhat dependent on me, or mold himself after me?

6. Can I let myself enter fully into the world of his feelings and personal meaning and see these as he does? Can I step into his private world so completely that I lose all desire to evaluate or judge it? There is a strong temptation to set students "straight," or to point out to a staff member the errors in his thinking. Yet when I can permit myself to understand in these situations it is mutually rewarding. . . .

7. Still another issue is whether I can be acceptant of each facet of this other person which he presents to me. Can I receive him as he is? Can I communicate this attitude? Or can I only receive him unconditionally, acceptant of some aspect of his feelings and silently or openly disapproving of other aspects? It has been my experience that when my attitude is conditional, then he cannot change or grow in respects in which I cannot fully receive him. . . .

8. Can I act with sufficient sensitivity in the relationship that my behavior will not be perceived as a threat?

9. Can I free him from the threat of external evaluation? In almost every phase of our lives—at home, at school, at work—we find ourselves under the rewards and punishments of external judgments. "That's good"; "that's naughty." "That's worth an A"; "that's a failure." Such judgments are a part of our lives from infancy to old age. I believe they have a certain social usefulness to institutions and organizations such as schools and professions. Like everyone else I find myself all too often making such evaluations. But, in my experience, they do not make for personal growth and hence I do not believe that they are a part of a helping relationship. . . .

10. Can I meet this other individual as a person who is in the process of becoming, or will I be bound by his past and by my past? If I accept the other person as something fixed, already diagnosed and classified, already shaped by his past, then I am doing my part to confirm this limited hypothesis. If I accept him as in process of becoming, then I am doing what I can to confirm or make real his potentialities.[1]

A Goal Worth Pursuing

Establishing a pastoral relationship with a couple is a goal worth striving for, even if you should not be able to do much to achieve the other purposes of the premarital sessions. With many couples, premarital preparation may be like an annual medical checkup, rather than problem-centered counseling. They may come to a group or to couple counseling with an adequate understanding of the nature of marriage, so that you feel you are not able to make much of a contribution. You may not need to give much specific help either. Each partner may already know fairly well what he or she brings to marriage as a person. The couple may be reasonably realistic about the adjustments they will be making in marriage. They may be aware of their weak points and be working on these. And they may be making good use of their strengths. You may discover that they are already communicating with each other in depth and are using their skills in problem-solving. But if you do nothing more than establish a relationship with the couple, we believe the premarital sessions will be worth all the time and energy they take.

Beyond what it does to facilitate interaction in group work and the counseling process itself, why is establishing a pastoral relationship so significant?

When such a relationship has been established, you are more available to the couple if later pastoral care or marriage counseling is needed. To be sure, you are supposed to be always available. But after an encounter in premarital counseling, you are emotionally available at a much deeper level. The doors are already open psychologically. The bridge is there to be used.

To some extent a good relationship may be carried over from one pastor to another. From a good experience in preparation for marriage, couples may generalize that pastors care about persons and their marriages, and are capable of giving help. Unhappily, the opposite is also true. Pastors who do not take their premarital preparation seriously give the impression that pastors do not care, that they are inept in ministering to marital needs.

The effort to establish a pastoral relationship may have value even when a couple resists premarital counseling. One pastor knew about a couple's approaching marriage several weeks before the wedding. But he was unable to get them to come in for counseling until he practically refused to perform the ceremony unless they did. They were both members of the church he was serving and residents of the neighborhood. At the pastor's insistence they came in very reluctantly the night before the wedding. The pastor did the best he could for them in the two-hour period they had.

He saw them together for about half an hour going over the marriage ritual in an effort to help them understand the meaning of the vows they were about to take. The woman entered into the discussion as much as she could and tried to encourage the man to participate. But she was obviously embarrassed that he refused to comment except to answer yes or no to direct questions.

Then the pastor saw each of them alone for half an hour, the man first. Even in the private interview the man said very little more than in the opening session. The pastor admitted his own discomfort and tried to reflect what he thought the man was feeling in the strained situation, but to no avail. In her private session the woman talked a little more freely, but only superficially. The pastor was aware of a major problem, but did not probe for it. She never brought it up.

The situation was not much improved in the last thirty-minute session with the couple together. Yes, they planned to be active in their new church after marriage. They wanted to start a family in a year or so, and she would see her doctor for birth control information. They thought they could handle their finances without any help from the pastor. And that was about it. To say the least, the pastor was very discouraged about these attempts at premarital counseling. He even wondered if it would have been better not to have insisted on going through the formality. But he had tried—perhaps too hard, he thought.

After the wedding the couple moved out of the city to a small town about fifty miles away, where the husband was principal of a small school. They came back home on holidays and attended church when there. But they had only casual contacts with the pastor for the next two years, mostly just speaking to him as they left the morning worship service.

After they had been married about two years, one day the husband surprised the pastor by calling for an appointment for himself and his wife. Verbal communication had almost broken down between them, and they thought it might help if the pastor would see them. They came for appointments almost every Saturday for about three months, during which time they made considerable progress.

As they came to the last session, it was the man who thanked the pastor and laughed about how different these sessions had been from premarital counseling. The pastor halfway apologized for forcing the premarital interviews. The man responded, "But you know, Pastor, I don't think I would have called you for this counseling if you hadn't insisted on seeing us before we married."

In the next chapter, we turn specifically to the practice of premarital counseling. We begin with educative counseling, and we will consider problem-centered counseling in chapter 11.

Chapter 10
Educative Counseling

The earlier parts of this manual apply to both group preparation for marriage and premarital counseling with a couple. In this part we now focus specifically on the practice of premarital counseling.

Premarital counseling (within the context of pastoral counseling) is *a process in which a pastor helps one or more persons or couples, or their families, to review their readiness for marriage, to make plans, and to solve problems in the area of preparation for marriage.*[1]

This manual is concerned primarily with premarital counseling between a pastor and a couple who are actually in the process of preparing for marriage and planning for the wedding, which the pastor will conduct. It assumes that both the man and the woman are available for the counseling. At times, however, one of them may be unavailable, as when the man is in military service. Another exception is the engaged couple who may be evaluating their relationship and who may decide not to marry.

On occasion, premarital counseling may include persons other than the couple. For example, parents of the couple may be a part of the process when there are special problems such as premarital pregnancy, or when the couple is very young. At times certain individuals may seek premarital counseling. A person who has no immediate plans for marriage may still want to know the meaning of marriage if marriage is a future possibility. Or a person who has been "jilted" may need help in adjusting to "no marriage." As a pastor you may also work with several couples in group premarital preparation, as already indicated.

Teaching and Counseling

The above definition of premarital counseling is an umbrella statement covering both the instructional aspects, called educative counseling,[2] and the person-initiated, problem-centered aspects of pastoral counseling.[3] In this chapter we explore some of the educative aspects of premarital counseling. In the next chapter we discuss problem-centered counseling.

Structure

For most pastors, premarital counseling is an integration of both their teaching and their counseling functions. The basic structure, content, and process of premarital counseling are derived primarily from the educative aspects of the process.

By structure we mean the overall framework of the premarital counseling sessions within which a pastor and a couple explore various areas of concern. To illustrate: As pastor you may follow a basic pattern of four one-hour interviews. First you see the couple together. In the next two interviews you have an individual appointment with each partner. In the fourth interview, you see them together again (for greater detail, see chapters 12 to 15 on procedures and resources). This pattern is called basic because it is the usual arrangement. However, it may be changed by adding other sessions whenever an individual or a couple need more counseling than this pattern specifies.

The first interview is structured to establish a free and open relationship—a primary counseling goal—as soon as possible. In most situations this is also the time to take care of certain items of information regarding the wedding plans (see the Wedding Information form in the back of the couple's workbook). Primarily, however, the purpose of this first session is to explore with the couple their understanding of the nature of marriage and the meaning of the vows they are assuming, and to try to determine where they are in their preparation for marriage. These goals are basically educational in nature.

The private interviews may be structured around the concerns the couple bring to marriage as individuals—their personalities, backgrounds, values, and so forth—and probably some of the areas of adjustment that are easier to talk about in private than in joint sessions; such as compatibility, sex, or in-laws. In most cases these subjects may be initiated in the private sessions and followed up in the couple session.

In the final joint interview, you and the couple may discuss certain developmental tasks or plans for adjustment in marriage, such as planning for children, earning and spending their money, developing a common philosophy or religion. These areas of concern are content areas and hence educational.

Flexibility

We would like to emphasize that such a structure must be flexible in order to give more attention to issues or concerns where there is greater need, or to exclude altogether areas where there is little or no need. This structure must also be flexible enough to allow the basic framework of interviews to be changed at any time; whenever a problem emerges that calls for further counseling. Such a problem, and the counseling called for, may be handled in the regular interview time. Or one or more additional appointments may be added, for the individual alone or for the couple.

You may find it difficult to know when you are doing educative counseling and when you are doing problem-centered counseling, since premarital counseling is such a mix of the two. Actually, premarital counseling is an integration of the two, or it may continually shift from one to the other. A clear understanding of both kinds of premarital counseling should help you function more skillfully in each and, therefore, be of more help to a couple.

Some pastors make the mistake of trying to conduct all joint interviews as educative counseling and all private appointments as problem-centered counseling. If you do this, you may run into real difficulty when a problem arises in the joint interview that calls for further counseling, or in the private appointment if the person does not mention any problems.

Usually the private interview is mostly instructional. For example, you may respond to the questionnaire request for sex information by ex-

plaining the nature of the reactions of the opposite sex or giving suggestions about intercourse, when that is requested. On the other hand, in the middle of a joint interview the process may change. You may be talking with a couple about the importance of seeing a physician for their premarital medical consultation and may sense a sudden embarrassment and reticence in them about talking about it. Without probing, you may express their feeling that the subject is difficult to talk about. The couple may feel enough understanding and support to tell you that they think the woman is pregnant. Suddenly the situation shifts from educative to problem-centered counseling.

To respond to this kind of situation you need to be sensitive as well as flexible. Try to be sensitive to a need whenever it arises. This does not mean that you are forever suspicious, always expecting something to happen and therefore always probing for problems. But it does mean that you will do your best to be keenly aware of any change of feelings whenever the atmosphere becomes charged with emotion, or when one person gives the other a negative signal of any kind. Be careful not to be so preoccupied with your own (educative) agenda that you are unaware of what is going on between the partners.

Similarly, whenever a problem arises, you need to be ready to shift roles immediately. Again you must not be so obsessed with your agenda that you cannot drop it and move with the couple to their chief concern at the moment.

Content and Process

In its educative aspects, premarital counseling has a content—something previously experienced or understood by others, which may be shared with, or made available to, a couple. This content includes not only information, experience, and skills, but also principles, values, and beliefs. Some of this content may be recorded in books, films, tests, and so forth. It may also be in your mind and experience, or in the persons you counsel—something they have learned (facts, skills) or have committed themselves to (values, beliefs).

The basic body of this content is suggested in Part II, Purpose and Content, and in chapter 3, "Toward a Theology of Marriage." The word "suggested" is used advisedly, for the content is outlined only briefly in this manual. For a fuller coverage of the recorded content, refer to the books listed in the Bibliography. A wise pastor never tries to review the entire content with any one couple. They may not want to know that much about it! And it would take more time than you can give to do it. This means that you will be very selective in your use of content, matching available knowledge to the needs of the person or couple.[4]

Even in its educative aspects, premarital counseling is much more than information-giving, although this is an important part of the process. We hope you will not hesitate to give information when this is needed. The most common procedure in this aspect of premarital counseling is for the pastor to stimulate conversation with the couple by asking questions. These questions can be nonthreatening, yet reveal the present state of the couple's preparation and readiness for marriage.

What is recommended here is not probing, for probing intrudes into the inner world of the person and usually concerns thoughts, attitudes, feelings, or experiences that the person may not wish to reveal to others. This questioning is a process in which you take the initiative, but you do not hesitate to yield that initiative to one or both of the partners when they are ready to move into other areas of concern.

Process

The educative part of premarital counseling is characterized by a process in which you function in a way different from that used in problem-centered counseling. This process usually involves four steps.

1. *Review readiness.* Educative counseling in premarital counseling is a process in which you help persons or couples review their readiness for marriage. In this review, you may guide them in both an exploration and an evaluation of their understanding of the nature of marriage, their knowledge of what they bring to marriage as persons, the adjustments they are making with each other as they prepare for marriage, and their plans for making their adjustments (or achieving their developmental tasks, as discussed in chapter 15) after marriage.

2. *Identify needs.* In the midst of this review you can assist persons or couples to identify and assess their needs related to preparation for marriage. These include their immediate needs as individuals or as engaged couples in their present relationship. These needs also include their anticipated needs in the adjustments they will have to make in marriage. They may be aware of some of these needs, such as understanding how to adjust sexually or how to manage their money. They may be able to identify these rather easily through responding to a few questions, either verbally or in writing (see the

premarital questionnaires in the couple's workbook). But they may not be aware of other needs you may have in mind, such as the need for an understanding and acceptance of marriage as a covenant relationship.

In assessing needs, you and the couple together choose to work on certain needs in the counseling process itself. You might decide to leave others for the couple to do on their own. You might help them to weigh carefully the relative seriousness of each need. The couple might want to work on those areas which seem most urgent to them at the moment. In this sorting process, however, you will need to guide the couple in balancing the urgency of certain needs with their ability to use available information, values, and so forth.

3. *Discover resources.* Next, you can help the couple discover methods and resources to meet these needs. Much of this will be done in conversation as you meet with them individually and together. If, for example, their need is for greater communication in certain areas of disagreement, you may actually guide them into the experience of examining each other's point of view and working through to some form of mutually agreeable solution. It may be necessary for you only to start the process during an interview and to let them continue it on their own.

On the other hand, some couples will require the services of other professional persons. All couples should see a medical doctor for their premarital medical consultation. A very few may need to see a psychologist for personality testing. No doubt you will want to recommend certain basic reading for most couples, as suggested in the Bibliography. For others, additional books or selected chapters may be suggested that deal with specific areas of need.

4. *Make plans.* Finally, you may help the couple utilize the appropriate methods and resources and make plans for their life together. This is a positive effort to undergird the possibility that the insights, information, and values discovered in premarital counseling actually be used to benefit the marriage. Encourage the couple to use these new understandings in specific plans they are making, so that premarital counseling "does some good."

Usually it is not enough simply to suggest certain reading, as relevant as this may be. You may need to check with the couple to see how much they have assimilated. You may find it necessary to point out certain information or principles that you think have significance for them and to assist them in using these in specific planning.

A case in point is the budget. For most couples,

reading a chapter on money management does not give enough help. You may need to review with them the items and amounts proposed and to explore the practicality of these proposals. Together they may need to evaluate the way they plan to operate their financial spending—who does what and who is responsible to whom and for what.

In addition to referring a couple to a medical doctor, you will want to check with the couple to see what they have learned and how well they can utilize the information. Probably you will find it necessary to supplement the physician's counseling. For example, you may need to give some help in certain areas, such as attitudes toward sex or birth control.

Since most of what is recommended in the final four chapters on procedures and resources is primarily educative counseling, we turn to problem-centered counseling in the next chapter.

One of the functions of premarital counseling is to help persons solve problems in preparation for marriage. When seen from this perspective, *premarital counseling may be described as a personal and dynamic process in which a pastor and one or more persons, with mutual consideration for one another, approach a mutually defined problem, to the end that the person(s) be aided to a self-determined resolution of the problem.* The counselees should become more mature people, capable of sustaining more wholesome relationships, who in the future will be able to handle problems as they come along. Let us briefly examine each part of this definition.

This chapter is not an attempt to give a detailed description of the counseling process. Rather, this chapter is an effort to summarize some of the essentials of counseling and to relate them to premarital counseling as such. Problem-centered counseling usually calls for more time than the suggested four or five interviews.

This discussion primarily focuses on the person-initiated, problem-centered aspects of premarital counseling. But it also describes some elements of the total counseling relationship that serve as the framework for the entire premarital counseling process in both its problem-solving and educative aspects. Problem-centered counseling may occur in the midst of instructional counseling whenever a problem arises that the person or couple wishes to pursue further. Or it may happen when a person takes the initiative in seeking out the pastor for counseling because of an increasing awareness of a problem as the wedding date draws near.

This was the case with a young man who approached a pastor, other than his own, six months before his proposed wedding date. The young man held rather liberal theological views and was active in a liturgical church. For about a month he had been engaged to a young woman from a sectarian church. They became involved in a very upsetting argument when she insisted on their attending an all-night singing convention, and he refused. This argument brought out their theological differences. The young man felt that their entire relationship was threatened by their religious differences and wanted help. It is interesting that he chose to go to a pastor who he believed held liberal theological views.

A Personal and Dynamic Process

Premarital counseling is "a personal and dynamic process." It is not mechanical, but involves the face-to-face encounter of persons. Primarily this counseling is a personal relationship and not a set of techniques, although special methods are employed to facilitate the process.

Premarital counseling is also personal in the sense that each case is unique. Each person and each couple is different from all others and must be counseled on an individual basis. The counseling is personal also in the sense that you are dealing with people's intimate and private concerns.

Premarital counseling is dynamic, not static. This means that it is a moving interactive process and not a stationary situation. It is a relationship in which the pastor and the couple attempt to deal with all the forces at work in the situation, but especially with the feelings. Premarital counseling is dynamic because it stimulates growth and development. It has power to change lives and relationships.

This kind of counseling is a process in which feelings are expressed, understood, reflected, and responsibly faced, and in which problems are solved, decisions made, and actions taken.

"*A pastor and one or more persons*" are involved in

premarital counseling. As already indicated, premarital counseling may involve the pastor and only one person, or a couple, or other persons. On rare occasions there may be the "other woman" or the "other man" who has been jilted. More often the other persons will be members of one or both of the immediate families of the partners. When couples are very young, their parents may be involved. When the persons are in the later years of life, their grown children, who feel they have a stake in the marriage (and may oppose it), may be the other persons involved.

On a few occasions, one or more sessions of premarital counseling may become family counseling in which the pastor sees at one time not only the couple, but also both sets of parents.[1] For example, this was necessary in a situation where communication had almost completely broken down between a young couple and their parents. Both of the young people were twenty years old. The young man had one more year in college and his fiancée had two. When they insisted on getting married within three months, both sets of parents said no and refused to talk about any plans for a June wedding. But the young people were determined to go ahead with their plans with or without parental consent.

It was the young woman's mother who asked the pastor to see the couple. She hoped he could "talk them out of it." The pastor said he would be happy to see them if they wanted to come in. He warned the mother that he would not tell them what to do but assured her he would help them review their readiness for marriage. The young people were willing to come in, for they hoped the pastor could help them secure their parents' approval.

The pastor saw the young people in four interviews, first together, then separately, and finally together again. He discovered that they were determined to go ahead with the wedding and were making responsible plans to that end. If their parents would not continue to finance their education, they planned for the woman to drop out of college and take a secretarial job until her husband graduated the following year. When he was able to support them, she planned to finish her education. This meant waiting more than three years to have children, and she had already seen her doctor and made plans to start on the Pill in another month. The couple evidenced genuine concern for their parents' views and feelings, but felt there was no real reason for their opposing the marriage.

Between sessions with the young people the pastor saw both sets of parents separately, then together. The families had been friends for a number of years, and the young people had been dating more than two years. Interviews with the parents revealed their anxiety about the young people being "too young" and their desire to see them through college before marriage. They objected only to the timing of the wedding; they wanted the couple to wait two years. They also expressed some fear that the young woman might become pregnant out of wedlock if marriage was delayed that long.

The pastor felt the best way to resolve the impasse was to get all six persons together. They agreed. When counseling was started, there had been almost no communication between the young people and their parents. By the time they all came together, everyone was eager to talk. And each person was less insistent on her/his previous position and more ready to understand the others' point of view. In the hour-and-a-half session all the parents except the woman's father were convinced that the young people were making responsible plans and should be supported. The parents agreed to finance their education on the same basis as when they were single and to go ahead with plans for a June wedding.

Following this joint session, the pastor saw the woman's father alone for one more interview. He still felt that his "little girl" was too young to marry, but felt that he would have to go along with the others' decision, and he reluctantly agreed to their marriage. Some time later the pastor had three more sessions with the young people, seeing them separately and together, to further their marriage preparation.

In problem-centered counseling the pastor and the person(s) "approach *a mutually defined problem*." It is essential that the problem be clearly defined. If an individual, with the help of the pastor, is still unable to identify and describe the problem, such a person may not be a proper candidate for counseling with a pastor. The difficulty may be in the unconscious mind and the person may therefore need the services of a psychiatrist. In such instances, of course, a referral should be considered. Whenever possible, however, the pastor should consult a psychiatrist who can give guidance for further exploration with the person before actual referral is made. This is one of many reasons why we recommend that you maintain a continuing consulting relationship with a psychiatrist or a marriage counselor supervisor, if at all possible.

It is also essential that the pastor and the person agree on what the problem is. If they are unable to agree on the nature of the problem, they may be working on different levels, or even different problems, and actually miss each other in the process.

One pastor discovered that this was exactly what he had done. A woman came to see him. He was the pastor of the church she had been attending for about a year in the large city where she worked. She was engaged to a man who was in military service and unavailable for counseling. They were to be married in her hometown by the local minister in two months. This woman came to the pastor wanting to know how she could get her fiancé to agree to a large church wedding, as he preferred a brief ceremony in the pastor's study.

As she talked, the pastor discovered that she was a rather domineering person. In his own mind he identified the problem as growing out of the woman's trying to control the couple's total relationship. So he did his best to get her to be more understanding of her fiancé and to give him more freedom to be himself. After three interviews she thanked the pastor for what he had done, but said there was just one question she wished he could help her with: "How can I get my fiancé to agree to a church wedding?"

In counseling it is necessary to begin with the present problem, mutually agreed upon, and to work on that until the couple together or the individual agrees to move to another problem. Otherwise, very little progress can be made.

Another essential condition to problem-centered counseling is *mutual consideration*. Mutual consideration moves in both directions—the pastor's attitude toward the person, and the person's attitude toward the pastor. As already indicated, the pastor is one who cares, respects, accepts, and affirms the person in counseling.

This consideration may be expressed by your not being shocked or repelled by anything the person or couple reveal, not because you are unfeeling, but because your concern for these people is so strong and genuine that you feel with and for them regardless of what they have done before. You do not judge or condemn persons but accept them as they are. They are not manipulated or told what to *do;* instead, their freedom and sense of responsibility are respected. You treat them as autonomous persons.

This consideration is also expressed when you *keep confidences*. You keep confidences because of your respect for persons and also because you know it is essential if counseling is to reach any significant depth.

A farmer in his late twenties had been seeing his pastor, trying to decide whether or not to become engaged to the woman with whom he had been going steady for more than two years. He was an active member of the church and a close friend to the pastor and his wife. He had asked the pastor to tell his wife about the counseling sessions. The pastor told his friend that he made it a practice not to share such information with anyone, not even his wife.

On his way to the fourth interview the farmer took a basket of vegetables to the parsonage and said something to the pastor's wife about seeing the pastor for counseling. He discovered that she did not know anything about it, that the pastor actually had kept their counseling relationship confidential. It was no coincidence that in the fourth session the farmer began to talk about his homosexual orientation. The pastor believes that the man never would have mentioned his homosexuality if the pastor's wife had known about the counseling sessions.

For any significant counseling to take place, it is also necessary for the person to show some *consideration for you as pastor*. In some instances it may be necessary for you to help persons understand what form this consideration ought to take. You have an opportunity to help them accept you as a pastoral counselor and not to expect you to be a psychiatrist or anyone other than the minister of the gospel that you are. For example, if transference in the psychoanalytic sense occurs, and the person unconsciously relates to you as if you are some significant person from childhood; unless you are trained in psychotherapy, you need to direct the relationship back to the conscious level. If you are unable to do this, we recommend that you consider a psychiatric referral for the person, or at least consult a psychiatrist to help you understand and learn.

Persons seeking help also must be willing to work within the limits of the counseling relationship. This generally means that counseling must be confined to the sessions agreed upon. They must not make unreasonable demands on you through numerous telephone calls or during chance encounters at various church meetings. They must accept you as a counselor who helps them make their own decisions, but who does not take over their responsibility for themselves.

This means that you will need to be aware of what is happening so that you will not be manipulated or controlled by persons you are counseling. Trying to get you to take sides when there are conflicts is one of the most common forms of manipulation. Perhaps this was one reason the young man with liberal theological views, who was engaged to the gospel-singing woman from a conservative church, sought out a pastor with liberal views. Of course he may have chosen the particular pastor because he was known to be a good counselor. But the pastor himself reported that the young man made several attempts to secure agreement with his position and to get the woman to change her views. The pastor refused to let himself be used in this manner and insisted that the couple make their own decisions. In the process, each of them made some concessions, and together they worked out a compromise both of them could live with.

Self-determined Resolution

One of the pastor's main purposes in problem-centered counseling is to help the person reach a *"self-determined resolution of the problem."* This is the heart of successful counseling, in that the pastor is a helper more than a leader, a servant instead of a ruler.

As we have said throughout this book, the pastoral counselor is one who assists a person or a couple in making decisions or plans. As such a helper you may guide them through the five basic stages of the problem-solving process as outlined, but leave the actual choice of action to them. At no stage in the process do you take over their responsibility. Instead, you function as a facilitator; not hindering or obstructing progress in decision-making and planning, but easing the pressures and making the process less difficult.

The counselor is also an enabler. You provide the opportunity for something to happen, the atmosphere in which it is easier to share. You offer the means by which problem solving may be facilitated. You give encouragement and support to strengthen a couple in their planning. You can make suggestions, but they are free to accept or reject them. You can point out certain facts or forces you think they are overlooking, but you let them decide what to do about these facts. In short, you help them make a self-determined resolution of their problem.

Many pastors, however, make the mistake of trying to do too much for couples they marry. The fear of failure often may cause a pastor to overdo it. If the pastor is obsessed with the necessity to succeed, he or she may be afraid to let a couple make their own decisions. We believe a couple needs to have the freedom to fail, and that you can do your best work when you give them that freedom. Otherwise, they are not really free. We simply remind you that everything does not depend on you, and we believe you can trust God to work in the lives of the two persons entirely apart from your efforts.

The resolution of a problem may be its actual solution. On the other hand, it may mean accepting the fact of a difference and deciding to be willing to live with it. Or, it may be acknowledging the fact that a condition will continue to exist and learning how to cope with it. Ideally, the resolution of problems in premarital counseling is some form of mutually satisfying agreement between the persons counseled.

Beyond problem-solving, as important as that is, a greater concern is that premarital counseling will help couples *"become more mature persons"* in the process. The way you conduct the counseling sessions—the way you help a couple solve their problems—determines whether they become dependent on you or are strengthened to work out their lives together. This is why so much has been said in the foregoing paragraphs about your being careful to help people arrive at a self-determined resolution of their problems.

To be sure, premarital counseling is not strictly insight counseling, for that takes a long time, more time than the limited number of sessions usually allows. But some clearer self-understanding should result for the persons being counseled. To be sure, emphasis is usually placed on problems in the couple's relationship, rather than on personal problems; but, to some extent, persons may become more mature and responsible in the process.

In spite of the limitations of premarital counseling that must be recognized, we believe that counseling can help individuals gain sufficient ego strength, self-understanding, and courage to risk an openness with each other that they have not known before. At least it can help persons move in this direction.

Premarital counseling can also contribute to a person's growing sensitivity to the partner's needs and can stimulate a willingness to respond with sympathetic understanding and love. If all this can be done, you are not only helping them to solve problems, you are helping persons mature according to God's purposes for them.

No doubt you are also concerned about helping persons to become *"capable of sustaining more wholesome relationships."* Certainly you would not be interested in premarital counseling unless you believed that it could bring some improvement to the relationship of the couple, insofar as this is possible under the time limitations. In facing their differences and the accompanying tensions, the couple may begin to come to terms with their need for both intimacy and distance, and begin to find some mutually satisfying balance.

Even though the process will continue throughout the marriage, premarital counseling may sensitize two persons to the significance of each partner's granting the other the freedom to be an individual, while at the same time being related in such deep intimacy that each truly knows the other. As a man and a woman work out their problems together, we can hope they will discover that their marriage is a relationship that cannot be taken for granted, but is one that must be nourished and cultivated in order to grow and enrich their lives through the years. Premarital counseling cannot assure success, but it can help a couple to make a start in the right direction and trust God for further guidance.

Finally, problem-centered counseling is a means of facilitating growth in persons so that *"in the future they will be able to handle problems as they come along."* Couples are strengthened to stand on their own feet and to live their own lives, instead of being made more dependent on their pastor.

Although as their pastor you want to always be available when you are actually needed, the couple should not feel that they have to return to you every time a new problem arises. They should have developed enough inner strength as persons, grown enough in their relationship with each other, and learned enough of the skills of problem-solving that they will be able to tackle their problems themselves.

Some pastors, however, have such a strong desire to be needed that they encourage dependency. Such pastors feel "left out" when couples are able to work out their problems. Actually, this skill in problem-solving should be a cause for rejoicing by both the couple and the pastor.

One pastor reported that a couple became so dependent on him that they returned for counseling almost every time even a minor problem came up. Before the end of their first year of marriage they had seen their pastor in four or five series of counseling sessions about finances, relatives, sex, work, and planning for children. He indicated that he did his best to get them to make their own decisions, but they kept coming back to him.

Shortly after their first anniversary the pastor moved to another church several hundred miles away. Both husband and wife were in tears in their anxiety over losing their counselor. They actually told him they were afraid they would not be able to work out their problems without his help. After he had been gone for about three months the pastor received a letter from the husband, apologizing for having depended on him so much, and saying that they were doing very well on their own now. "In fact," the man wrote, "I guess your leaving town was about the best thing that has happened to our marriage!"

In the next four chapters we present a model from which you may develop your own plan of premarital counseling—one that seems most appropriate for you. You will want to take your time and energy and skill into account, as well as a couple's readiness and need. Some pastors may feel that the plan given here is too idealistic. We see it as a basic minimum program of premarital counseling as part of an overall marriage preparation plan.

For a variety of reasons you will find situations in which four or five interviews with every couple will not be possible. On the other hand, this basic pattern will not be enough for some of you. You may already be giving more than four or five hours to each couple you marry. What we recommend here is a basic plan that can be expanded as the needs of a particular couple indicate.

A minimum of five interviews is recommended as the usual procedure with most couples. Here is a brief overview. In the first interview, the pastor sees the couple together. In the next two, each person is seen separately. They are together again for the fourth. The fifth interview is to be scheduled by the couple from one to six months after the wedding (in addition to these counseling sessions, remember we are recommending that couples attend a marital growth group during their first year of marriage). Suggested procedure for conducting each of these interviews will be described in some detail.

Encourage Early Contact

Couples should be encouraged to begin premarital counseling at least six weeks to three months before the wedding. The best time is before the engagement, or as soon thereafter as possible, especially if the couple needs to face any serious limitations in their relationship.

Many of you will learn about a couple's wedding plans only a few days before the event, and will be forced to do the best you can in the limited time available. How can couples be encouraged to make early contact?

If you are a married man (though we realize many of you are not), your wife may give invaluable help. Often she is the first to learn that a wedding is coming up. One of the women in the church may share the news that "my daughter is engaged," or the young people may know your wife so well that they confide in her about their wedding plans. Or a telephone call may be received at the parsonage—a query as to your availability for a wedding at a specified time. This is more apt to happen in churches that do not employ a secretary.

A pastor's wife may handle such contacts as a daily routine, simply as a matter of scheduling an event on the church calendar. On the other hand, she may use them as a means of helping the couple anticipate premarital counseling. She can let it be known that you would like to see the couple as soon as possible to help them prepare for marriage, and she can find out how you can contact them. If you have a secretary, it is important, whenever a call comes to the church, that the secretary do the same thing.

You can build a network of communication by alerting parents, teachers, and young adults of your interest in learning about any engagements. You may want to put a note of congratulations and best wishes in the church newsletter or bulletin whenever you learn about an engagement—with the permission of the couple, of course. Most couples appreciate this kind of recognition by the church, and it is one way for the church to let the couple know it cares about them. If it is done for one couple, others begin to let the church know when they want their engagement announced.

You may give the couple a book on the meaning of marriage as soon as you hear they are engaged. The word soon gets around among the young people of the church that the pastor has a good book on marriage. This encourages early contact with you.

Some of the most effective ways of encouraging early contact are open to you as pastor. As suggested in chapter 4, whenever possible you may be involved in special study courses for young people on preparation for marriage.[1] In these courses you can explain what you do in premarital counseling and give some of the reasons why early contact is so important. Sermons on marriage and family life are another way to point out the value of early contact in preparing for marriage.

Early contact can be encouraged through printed materials. A church library can contain some of the best books on preparation for marriage. You can see that these carry an insert from you, indicating your desire to be of service to all young people planning to be married and your desire to see couples as early as possible. The distribution of pertinent leaflets for both young people and their parents may also encourage early counseling sessions.

Many churches are now preparing and circulating policy statements about weddings. Certainly such statements should include your policy about premarital counseling. These might be printed in the church bulletin or newsletter to inform the congregation.

Because so much happens during each interview, we strongly urge you to *keep a written record* of each session. During the interview you may make a rather sketchy account by jotting down key words or topic sentences. After the session you can fill in with more complete statements.

It is unwise to try to remember without written notes all that happens in each session. There is too much danger of forgetting some essential details or of confusing one person or couple with another. With certain couples these records might be of value, not only in the immediate interviews, but also in any counseling sessions you might have months or even years later.

Of course any records must be kept confidential. No names or other identifying information should be included. Instead, code numbers can be used, just as on the premarital questionnaires in *Preparing for Christian Marriage*. Instead of using names, a man may be identified as Mr. X and a woman as Ms. Y.

In the first interview we recommend that you see the couple together. Why is this better than seeing them separately?

One of the basic reasons is to get them started together. This protects each partner from any feeling that you have set up an alliance with the other one. This precaution may be crucial if one is from another town or another church. It is important that they both feel they are making their preparations together. This also makes it possible for them to decide together whether they will continue with the additional counseling sessions.

Having them come together means that you identify them as a couple. This minimizes any feelings of separation or isolation, and may be especially significant if there is a problem in any aspect of their relationship. Being together may make it easier for them to focus on their relationship, for the relationship is present only when both partners are present.

Two persons support each other by their very presence. Together they are likely to feel more comfortable in seeing you for the first time for counseling. They are usually uncertain enough about counseling and anxious enough about getting married, without having to cope with the feeling of aloneness too.

Interviewing the couple together also gives you an opportunity to observe their relationship to each other, rather than observing them only as individuals. By seeing them together you may pick up clues about the way they relate to each other.

Perhaps the most important reason for seeing them together at first, however, is because of what happens to the couple as they share the experience. Each may stimulate the other to make particularly significant responses. They may raise questions with each other that deepen the process of preparation. This kind of exchange is likely also to stimulate better communication outside the counseling sessions.

At least six or seven things can happen in the first interview. Not all of these will be achieved completely, but the process can begin, and be well under way, before the end of the first session.

1. You can begin to establish a counseling relationship with the couple, and achieve some measure of rapport (see chap. 9). Without this rapport, nothing of any real significance is likely to happen in any of the sessions. You can provide a climate of trust in which open communication can take place. This climate depends, primarily, on the kind of person you are—caring, respecting, accepting, affirming—but also on the kind of response the couple makes to you. To a lesser extent, it depends on what you do and how you do it: the way you listen, understand, and respond to the couple and to

their feelings, the way you ask questions and respond to their answers.

2. It is your responsibility to structure the counseling sessions by letting the couple know what to expect, both in the immediate interview and in the following sessions. It will be best if you provide this structure through a process of negotiation with the couple, rather than dogmatically insisting that they follow a previously established plan. However, without some sense of organization supporting them, many persons are likely to feel at sea in the new experience of a permissive counseling relationship. Along with the flexibility and freedom, they need to feel that what is happening is part of a plan, and that there is some direction to it. They need to have some reassurance that you know what you are doing and where they are going.

3. You can help a couple begin to review and evaluate the preparation they have already made for marriage. (For more detail on this and the next two items, see p. 55).

4. You can also help them identify and assess their need for further preparation, both as individuals and as a couple, as much as possible.

5. Based on this review and assessment, you might suggest appropriate resources or methods for meeting their needs.

6. One of the most important concerns in this first interview is helping the couple to understand the covenantal nature of marriage from the Christian perspective.

7. In most instances plans are made for the rehearsal and the wedding (and possibly for some appointments after the wedding).

It may seem that this is a great deal to do in one interview, and it is. This is one reason the first session should be scheduled for an hour and a half, whereas the other appointments are usually limited to one hour each. The first interview is only one step in a longer process, with at least three more sessions suggested before the wedding.

One of the first things to do is to help the couple feel at ease with you and relax as much as possible. A good way to do this is to encourage them to talk about how they feel about being there. Your helping them to be aware of their feelings and to express them may relieve some of their anxiety.

If one or both persons is a stranger to you, some time should be spent in getting acquainted. To do this, you may ask some simple, easily answered questions to find out what you can about them and their relationship, such as: How long have you known each other? How did you meet? When were you first sure that he/she was the one for you? When did you get engaged? In this way, you begin to share in their relationship. Let them know you have a genuine interest in them and their love for each other.

A good way to develop a counseling relationship is to *start at the point of the couple's interest.* If their chief concern is planning for the wedding, as is true for most couples, this is the place to begin. You will want to take enough time to answer their questions without any appearance of rushing, but at the same time be as brief as possible. Time can be saved if the couple fills out the wedding information blank in the back of the couple's workbook. However, because of the nature of some of the questions, this is best done at the end of the session. Or, the couple may take the blank with them, complete it, and return it to you later.

In this introductory period, you might want to ask about their reasons for asking a pastor to perform their ceremony. This could be especially significant if they are not members of your congregation. Discussing such a question may deepen your relationship. It could also give some clues about problem areas to be checked out later.

Caution is usually in order in this first interview. Probing for problems may threaten the counseling relationship. We have found that problems will surface at the appropriate time, provided a sound relationship is established, and if the couple feels confident that you will not pressure them to reveal more than they are ready to share.

Review Their Preparation

Also in the first session, you will want to find out what preparations a couple have already made for marriage. This information can guide you in suggesting further steps to be taken. What courses in marriage and family life have they had in high school or college? What reading have they done? How much, and at what level (find out authors and titles, if possible)? How helpful do they feel their reading has been? Answers to questions such as these serve as guides to additional reading that you might recommend (see p. 64 for basic recommendations and the Bibliography for others).

It is helpful to know what counseling they have had with other professionals. A crucial question is: Have you seen your medical doctor yet? Since many couples will think of seeing their physician only to meet the legal requirements for a blood test, you may need to stress the value of a premarital medical consultation. This is the time to recommend a physician whom you know to be trained and competent to do this kind of work.

If time permits, the individual interviews can be scheduled in two weeks. This allows time for the couple to see a physician before the private appointments. It also leaves time for some of the reading. Scheduling the individual interviews after the visit to the physician gives you an opportunity to review what was done by the doctor and to supplement it if necessary. In addition, you may be able to help the couple assimilate and utilize information given by the medical doctor.

You should also check on some of the plans the couple are making for marriage, primarily to see where they are in their planning, rather than to give much specific help at this time. If a great deal of help is needed, additional counseling sessions need to be scheduled. Specific questions may be asked about such matters as plans for a place to live, work, finances, sharing household responsibilities, in-laws, friends, education, community activities, recreation, or religion.

Using the Questionnaires

One of the best ways to discover how to be of further help to a couple is to use the Premarital Questionnaires in the back of *Preparing for Christian Marriage*. Using the questionnaires will be helpful to you and the couple in several ways.

1. The questionnaires save time. In the twenty or thirty minutes it takes to fill out the forms, the couple give you information that would take four or five hours to share in conversation. At this stage, most couples are eager to save time. And of course you want to save time, too, without jeopardizing your usefulness to the couple.

2. The questionnaires give each person an opportunity to become involved, in a serious, systematic way, in marriage preparation—in reviewing their readiness for marriage and in identifying areas of need or further preparation. In filling out the questionnaires most persons discover items they had not thought important, and are motivated to work on them.

3. The questionnaires stimulate communication. Usually, just as soon as one of the couple completes the form, he or she is eager to know how the other person responded to certain items. Then the questions fly. "I didn't know you felt that way. I'd like to hear more about that." Real encounter may be under way—and most of it entirely outside the

appointed sessions. We think this is to be encouraged as long as they see it as constructive.

4. Use of the questionnaires also enables you to sort out a few major areas of need on which you can concentrate attention in the remaining interviews. They give you an overview of some pertinent influences in each person's background and some insights into the way they are adjusting to each other—strengths and weaknesses of the partners and of their relationship.

If *Preparing for Christian Marriage* has not been given to the couple previously, this should be done during the first interview. Some pastors prefer to remove the questionnaires from the couple's workbook before giving it to them. This makes it possible to separate the forms, and give them to each partner individually.

We think it is best to ask the couple to fill in the forms while they are in your office, perhaps at the end of the first interview. This insures that each person answers the questions alone, and that the questionnaires are left with you. If necessary, however, they can be taken home to be completed. If so, they can be enclosed in envelopes addressed to you so the couple can return them as soon as possible, at least the day before the next interview, to give you time to review them.

In any case, the partners should be carefully instructed to complete the forms according to the directions at the top of the first page. We think it is very important that each person fill out the questionnaire without help from the other. Once they have completed the forms, however, they should be encouraged to discuss them as much as they like.

Before giving out the questionnaires, you should fill in serial numbers for each person in the upper right-hand corner. You can identify each serial number by name and address in a confidential file. You may call attention to the fact that no names appear on the forms. This assures the couple that responses are confidential; they are for your use only. Of course you will discuss each person's questionnaire with that person in the private interview. Without violating confidences, you can also discuss issues raised by the fact that the partner gave different answers to the same questions.

Here are two ways this may be done in the individual interviews. First, in the area of background, question 5 may reveal a difference in religious outlook. You may simply ask the person to tell you how he or she feels about religious backgrounds, and take it from there.

A second approach may be in the area of

relationships. Question 27 is "Have you planned your budget?" Suppose the man answered yes and the woman no. Without telling the woman how her partner responded, you can say, "You indicated that you have not planned your budget. Can you tell me what you have talked about in the area of finances?"

She might reply, "Oh, yes, we've decided to have a budget, but we haven't decided on any amounts yet. We are not even sure what items should be included. Can you help us with that?"

You can give a positive response and suggest that they can best do that in the next joint interview. You can call attention to the suggestions in chapter 7 of *Preparing for Christian Marriage*. Or you can give her a budget form from which they can work out specific amounts. In the discussion you may discover that the man checked "yes" because they had decided to have a budget, and there may be no real conflict here. Yet further work is indicated both for the couple on their own and with you.

Review Both Questionnaires

Remember that you need to have both questionnaires returned to you in time to go over them carefully in preparation for the individual interviews. With some experience and careful concentration, we believe you can do this in fifteen to twenty minutes.

Privately you can check one form against the other, item by item, for agreements and differences. Agreements may indicate strengths that can be developed, and the differences, problems that require further attention. It saves time to make notes of items to be discussed in the margins of the questionnaires as you compare them. This is especially helpful when partners give different responses. You could use a different colored ink in making these notes.

Every question on the form is potentially important, but of course some are more significant than others as shown by the responses. The actual value of each question is closely related to the needs of the particular couple answering it. The significance of most of the questions is discussed in a number of college textbooks on education for marriage. You will find it helpful to be familiar with several of these in order to be aware of the potential significance of each question.

Because of their interrelatedness, some questions should be viewed in clusters; such as the marital status of the parents and condition of their marriages (questions 14 and 15), and those relating to the

individual's childhood (11, 12, 13, and 16). Such questions, however, must also be related to other factors, such as the person's education, especially if a functional course on preparing for marriage was included. Such a course, for example, might help to overcome some negative conditioning of childhood.

Other examples of clustering are found in those questions related to affection and sex (30 to 34) and disagreement (36 and 38). A particular question like number 26, on the wife's working, should be associated with another, like number 35 on planning for children, and number 34 on child-spacing.

In comparing one person's responses with the other's, questions such as number 28 on household responsibilities should be checked for differences and similarities in role expectation. Another example of related questions is number 29, on activities the couple participate in, and number 38 on disagreements. A good way to make this comparison is to copy the response of the partner onto each form, using a special symbol (such as "P" for partner) or a different colored ink.

Special attention is called to question 38 on areas of disagreement. A difference in the way each person checked a particular item could point to a lack of communication between them. Or it may indicate a difference in understanding the item, rather than a basic difference in views on this question. In our experience, many couples check for almost half the items in the first column, "the matter has not arisen," and almost half in the second column, "we agreed." For adequate marriage preparation, each of these items should be faced one way or another. Very few couples actually agree on all of these. But many persons come to marriage with only superficial consideration given to many of these items, and they are unaware of much difference. A little more depth exploration may show more disagreement.

In this connection, the last two columns under question 38 are very important. One person may feel that a particular item has been discussed only superficially, while the other rates it "discussed in depth." The person who rates a discussion as superficial may feel that a more thorough discussion is needed. Each area of disagreement should be noted and worked through.

Actually, a couple indicating much disagreement in several areas might have learned how to handle their differences and could be in a stronger position than some others who are not aware of their disagreement. Of crucial significance, of course, is the way disagreements are faced or settled (question 36). The premarital counseling session may be the occasion for learning more constructive ways of handling differences.

The pastor does most of the work suggested above between the first interview, when the questionnaires are given out, and the second and third sessions, when they are discussed with each person in the individual interviews (further reference to the use of the questionnaires will be made in the next chapter, which is on the individual interviews).

There is more work to be done, however, in the initial interview. Some pastors check on the couple's role expectations. Most pastors review the couple's understanding of the nature of Christian marriage and of the vows they will take. The possible interviews in the remainder of the premarital counseling process should be outlined and scheduled, and certain reading suggested.

Some pastors prefer to focus on husband and wife *role expectations*. A number of paper and pencil tests are available in this area. One that is recommended is "A Marriage Role Expectation Inventory" by Marie S. Dunn.[2] This inventory contains two forms, one for the man and one for the woman, to be filled out individually. Each form contains 58 statements of various roles of husbands and wives. Each person indicates the perceived level of agreement or disagreement with each statement. They can easily do this in an hour.

After you score the inventories, you may discover that a particular couple needs only a little help. Others might need a great deal of guidance in facing differing expectations. They might need help in recognizing their conflicting role expectations and the adjustments that may be necessary in their marriage.

The Meaning of Marriage

One way to find out a couple's understanding of marriage is to ask them to talk about what a religious ceremony or a church wedding means to them. Some will respond that they would not feel married otherwise. Some will be frank enough to admit that they do not care, but that their parents insist on it. Some will not know any special reason; they just think that is the way to get married.

The pastor may need to sharpen the issue by asking them what the difference would be between going to a justice of the peace or other civil servant, and coming to the church. This is one way to help them differentiate between a civil service that would join them in a legal contract, which may be dissolved on certain grounds, and a religious ceremony in which they commit themselves to a covenant relationship. This could open the way for a full discussion of their understanding of the religious significance of marriage. You may find it productive to refer them to chapter 11 in *Preparing for Christian Marriage* (see also chap. 3 in this book).

Another possible approach is to review the marriage service. Unless the words are reviewed carefully in the premarital counseling session, they may not be heard at the wedding.

Two weeks after a certain pastor had married Mary and John, he performed another ceremony at which John was an usher. During the reception, John quizzed the minister, "Did you use a service today different from the one you used at our wedding?" The pastor assured him that he had used the same ritual, word for word. John looked at him for a serious moment, then grinned. "No kidding!" he exclaimed. "Did I agree to all that?"

In the formality of the counseling session you have an opportunity to discuss the meaning of the service and the spiritual significance of marriage. We suggest you do this with each couple, even though this may have been considered in a group session.

You could begin by explaining to the couple that, as you read over the service with them, they need not worry about such details as where to stand, or when to join hands or exchange rings. You can assure them that instructions for all this will be given at the rehearsal. Now is the time to concentrate on the words, on what it means to be married according to these vows.

As you read the service through, the couple can be encouraged to interrupt at any point to ask questions or to make comments. After reading the service through slowly, ask if they have any questions. If not, you can point out several of the most important statements, or explain some of the symbolism in the service and discuss it with the couple.

Certainly you will do this in your own way. (Here we will use the traditional United Methodist service as an example.) But several key concepts can be emphasized, such as those mentioned on pages 31-32 and elaborated upon in chapter 3. Among these are the following:

1. *Covenant relationship.* "The holy covenant you are about to make, you do now declare before this company your pledge of faith, each to the other."

2. *Love and fidelity.* "Wilt thou love her (him), comfort her (him), honor and keep her (him), in sickness and in health; and forsaking all other keep thee only unto her (him) so long as ye both shall live?" ". . . live together in faithfulness . . ."

3. *Lifelong union.* "... so long as ye both shall live?" "... till death us do part."

4. *Vocation.* "... having duly considered ..." "... and if steadfastly you endeavor to do the will of your heavenly Father ..."

5. *Other elements* of Christian marriage. Personal commitment to God in Christ—"in the name of the Father, and of the Son, and of the Holy Spirit. ..." "... through Christ our Lord ..." A part of a Christian community—"in the presence of God ... before this company ..." "... through the Church of Jesus Christ Our Lord. ..." With concern for others, in service to the community and the world—"Thy kingdom come, thy will be done on earth as it is in heaven." The overall goal of their life together—"and live according to thy laws."

You might find that some couples want to make changes in the wording of the ceremony. Others want to write their own service. You will note that the couple's workbook suggests that they work out any changes with you. How do you feel about making such changes? Are there some items that you want to be sure to include?

Schedule Interviews

Before the first interview ends you need to make a tentative assessment of the couple's readiness for marriage and their need for further preparation. Based on this, and within the limits of time available, decide how many interviews to recommend. You could suggest the regular series of one private appointment for each partner and a joint session before the wedding, and one afterward.

If the need is indicated, you may recommend several additional appointments, either private or with both of them. Or you may prefer to leave the exact number of appointments open until after the private sessions. In any case, you need to schedule them with the couple and outline what can be done in these sessions. On the other hand, now or later, you may decide to suggest one or more referrals for either or both persons.

If your assessment of the couple causes you to question their readiness for marriage, this should be dealt with as soon as is appropriate (see p 32).

You can recommend additional reading based on your assessment of the couple's need for further preparation. This reading should be a part of the counseling process and not a substitute for it. Some reading may raise questions that should be discussed in the sessions.

When reading is used as a basis for discussion, couples are not as likely to put it off—and never get to it—as when left on their own. Also, such discussion has the possible value of alerting you to other areas in which they need more help. Many pastors or church libraries have a number of good books that can be let out on a loan basis. If you do not have them, we urge you to invest in a few books carefully chosen for this purpose. Be sure to keep your offerings updated, for newer and sometimes better books are coming out each year. We find it necessary to keep careful records of books on loan.

Before suggesting any additional reading, it is wise to find out just what reading a couple have already done. This may be only a few superficial magazine articles. On the other hand, some may have read the very book you offer, or something better.

This is what happened to one pastor who gave an eighteen-year-old girl, just finishing high school, a fairly simple book of about 125 pages. When he asked how helpful the book had been, he was surprised to hear her say, "Not much." She had already read, rather carefully, a 700-page college text by one of the leading authorities!

For younger couples you may find David Mace's *Getting Ready for Marriage* most appropriate.

Young adults of college age may appreciate a text like Hunt and Rydman's *Creative Marriage* or McCary's *Freedom and Growth in Marriage*.

A very good book is *Your First Year of Marriage* by Tom McGinnis. Although written for those just married, it has some suggestions on communication and problem-solving especially helpful to engaged couples.

The next step is to see the man and the woman in private interviews. And that is what we discuss in the next chapter.

The second and third interviews have much in common, and can be considered together here. These are the private appointments in which the pastor sees each person alone.

Since the woman is more likely to be a member of your local congregation, you are probably already acquainted with her, but maybe not with the man. If this is true, it is usually better to see the man first, unless there is some special reason for seeing the woman before seeing him. As a general rule, you should see the one you do not know as well. This gives you an opportunity to strengthen the relationship. If you are equally well acquainted with both persons, the order of the appointments can be a matter of convenience.

Why Private Appointments?

In the private appointments the major concern is still the marriage, but as seen from the individual's point of view. There are distinct advantages in seeing each person alone.

The private appointment is an opportunity for you to strengthen the counseling relationship with each of the partners as individuals. Here, more than in the joint interview, the individual may come to feel that "the pastor does care about me as a person—my feelings, my needs, my aspirations—as well as about our marriage."

Some sense of relationship has already been established in the first joint interview. However, in the individual interview you are making a new beginning on a one-to-one basis. This one-to-one relationship is very different from the pastor-couple relationship. Now you can concentrate your full attention on one person, and a deeper and more inclusive relationship is possible. Now the person is free to concentrate on her or his own feelings about

anything under consideration, and on helping you understand what he or she means, instead of wondering how the partner is interpreting everything that is said, as may have been done in the joint interview.

This session gives you an opportunity to get to know the individual as a person. You might want to recheck impressions gained in the previous joint interview.

This is also the most appropriate time to focus on the individual's preparation for marriage. All of the functions of premarital counseling can be carried out in the private session, but with special reference to the individual. This setting provides the opportunity for the individual, with your help, to review her or his own readiness for marriage. Together, the two of you can identify and assess the needs for personal growth or treatment or further preparation for marriage.

You can also recommend certain resources on marriage preparation for the individual, or help the person assimilate and use such resources.

The private appointment stimulates communication. The one-to-one relationship makes it easier for a person to bring up certain problems or issues that might be difficult to mention in the presence of the partner. Discussing these with you alone could strengthen the person to talk them through with the partner later.

The individual may need the pastor's help in learning how to improve communication and actually come to grips with the causes of a problem. A couple may have become so irritated by a particular unresolved issue that communication has broken down, at least in this area. By discussing the issue in the private session, you may be able to break the logjam.

In the private appointment you can raise the kinds

of questions that are less likely to come up in the joint interview. This can have the effect of stimulating further thought and discussion between the partners.

Certain subjects may be especially appropriate for consideration in the individual interviews. To be sure, most of these should be faced by the couple together. But it may be wiser to initiate discussion in the individual sessions. Among these are such subjects as helping the person understand what each individual brings to marriage as a person, and some aspects of adjustment that a couple may be too sensitive to talk about. These could include such subjects as personality characteristics, sex, and in-laws.

For example, a man who feels some resistance to his future in-laws might hesitate to bring this up in the joint interviews, but would feel fairly free to discuss it with the pastor alone. Or, a woman may be slow to get into any discussion that might imply she is inadequate for marriage, or that might be interpreted by the other person as a reflection on her.

Still another reason for the private appointment is that it facilitates the addition of interviews if some problem arises that calls for extending the counseling sessions. You can simply suggest one or more additional appointments. This is more likely to be accepted by the person as a logical extension of the present pattern.

On the other hand, if the usual pattern is for the pastor to see the couple together every time, it may be awkward to suggest a private session for one person. That person is likely to think there must be something terribly wrong with her or him that a private session is necessary.

Suggested Procedure

How do you go about realizing some of the possibilities in the individual interview?

Since you are aware of the fact that the individual appointment adds a new dimension to the counseling relationship, at the beginning of the session, do all you can to put the person at ease. In a warm and friendly manner, let the peson know that you are glad to see her or him and that you appreciate the privilege of sharing in this preparation for marriage.

Helping a person to be comfortable in the counseling session means being sensitive to the person's feelings, even if they are negative feelings of resistance to the counseling or to the pastor. Expressing these feelings brings them out into the open where they can be faced and talked about.

Frequently, negative feelings subside when they are expressed, not because they surface and then are brushed aside, but because the experience of hearing one's feelings responded to in this manner gives a person a sense of being understood and accepted. The resistance may have arisen originally because the person expected the pastor, not to be understanding, but rejecting.

Sometimes a person feels uncomfortable in counseling because he or she is uncertain about what is about to happen. This fear of the unknown can be allayed by your giving some structure to the session. You can indicate some of the purposes of this conference and point out some of the things that may be done. These might include reviewing the premarital questionnaire, checking on the visit with the physician, discussing the reading suggested earlier, or talking about specific subjects.

Within the framework, you can let the person decide where to begin. This opens the way for the individual to bring up any problem or issue that he or she wants to talk about. If nothing comes as a result of this suggestion, you might proceed with the questionnaire.

Premarital Questionnaires

In reviewing the Premarital Questionnaires, begin with the earlier questions about the individual's background. This helps you to understand the person while you are helping him or her understand what he or she brings to marriage. This review might also include a comparison of the significant factors concerning similar items on the partner's questionnaire, again without the violation of confidence.

Before the session begins, you can prepare for it by noting items that seem to call for more discussion. For a particular individual most of the items will not be important enough to mention. But seemingly inconsequential items can take on crucial significance because of the partner's response.

For example, there may be nothing unusual about the fact that a woman is twenty-two years old. But if her partner is forty-five, this calls for some consideration. If either person has been divorced, this should be checked out according to "church standards," as well as the personal needs of the couple. If one of the partners has been recently widowed, it could take more time to work through the grief problem than it would to deal with a divorce.

What is suggested here is that it is not enough to take the simple facts on the questionnaire at face value. It is the *meaning* of these facts to one or both persons that is important. For example, what is the meaning of the couple's religious and educational backgrounds? In many instances it could be enough for you to call attention to a certain response and ask what effect the person thinks this may have on the marriage.

Because of the possibility that some *background influences* might cause tension in marriage, some questions may need rather extended discussion. This would be true if a man with certain fixed ideas of husband-wife roles is marrying a woman who plans to work outside the home, as most wives do today (question 26). The man may be conditioned against housework (question 7), which he might have to share if his wife works (compare question 28). Or he may have strong feelings generally against women working (question 8), which he might have to learn to accept. This kind of situation should be faced and worked through in premarital counseling, perhaps first with the man alone and later with the woman, or with both of them together. If responses to question 9 on the questionnaires indicate a wide divergence in economic backgrounds, this may indicate the need for careful consideration.

Further exploration is called for when question 12 reveals an unhappy childhood. Or when the questions about one's parents (questions 14 to 16) report any negative conditioning. Exploration might also be needed when question 13 indicates "very few" friends, especially if the partner reports "many."

The private appointment might be the best setting for checking on *relationship questions,* such as number 24 on how well the partners get along with their prospective in-laws, and number 23 on the parents' feelings about the marriage. Special problems may be encountered if there is parental disapproval. These questions can take on special significance if the partner rated any one of them differently.

In this connection, also compare question 24 on one form with question 16 on the partner's form. This kind of comparison should be made, too, with question 29 on both forms. The important thing is not the activities in which the partners participate, but how they feel about their participation.

Special attention should be given to the questions on affection and sex, numbers 30 through 35. The other person's response should be compared for possible differences in number 30 on affection. These responses may indicate that further discussion is needed.

You may want to evaluate responses to number 31, on courses or reading for understanding sexual

relations, as a guide in recommending further reading. Questions 32 and 35 about parents' discussion and feelings about sex should be checked for possible negative influences. These, along with questions 34 and 35, are most important in alerting you to the need for help with sex information and attitudes.

Some young people still come to marriage with very little preparation in the area of sexual relations and without having had much help from their parents, especially parents who feel that sex should only be "tolerated." And yet our culture glorifies sex. No wonder many of our young people anticipate sexual relations in marriage with "mixed feelings" and are doubtful that their present knowledge of sex is adequate for marriage. Some persons, however, consider their knowledge of sex adequate for marriage (question 34) and then request additional help by checking several items in the last part of this question.

It is heartening to note that more than three-fourths of our ministers discuss *sexual relationships* with the couples they marry. You need to be prepared to provide information on all of the subjects listed under number 34. If you do not feel capable of discussing any one of these items, however, you may refer the person to a good book on the subject. Or you may be able to refer the person to a competent medical doctor or to a clinic on family planning (see earlier discussion on pp. 81-84).

Counseling with Those Previously Married

Some pastors make the mistake of thinking that a person who has been married before does not need premarital counseling, especially in the area of sex adjustment. Our experience indicates, however, that persons in the middle or later years need premarital counseling just as much as young adults—some need it even more.[1] To be sure, counseling regarding sex, as with any other concern, should be determined by the need of the particular person or couple.

A widower in his middle forties, who had been married for more than twenty years, came for premarital counseling in preparation for his second marriage. In filling out the premarital questionnaire he reported that he thought his knowledge of sex adequate for marriage. But on question 34 he checked the item on "Sex reactions of the opposite sex." In discussing this with him his pastor mentioned the importance of the clitoris. "Clitoris?" he inquired, "what's that?" When the pastor explained, he was thoughtful for a moment. Then he said, half-talking to himself, "Well, I wonder if that's why my first wife didn't like sex." He turned to the pastor wistfully, "I wish I had known that twenty-five years ago."

As indicated above, you can anticipate that three out of four persons approaching marriage today will need some help in preparing for sexual relations. Generally speaking, if a person needs more help in this area than can be given in thirty minutes, it is necessary to add one or more additional counseling sessions. For if more time is taken to discuss sex in the regular four- or five-hour session, other equally important areas may be neglected.

Sex Knowledge Inventory

The Sex Knowledge Inventory,[2] called SKI for short, is a good resource for the pastor. It has two parts. Form X is a set of eighty multiple-choice questions on sex, mostly on sexual relations. Form Y is a test on sexual vocabulary and anatomy. It contains drawings of male and female anatomy, with parts to be identified and functions described.

A few pastors use the SKI with almost all the couples they marry. But we recommend it for routine use only if a minimum of six or seven hours is allotted to premarital counseling. The reason for this is that it takes considerable time to administer and interpret.

To be administered properly the SKI needs to be taken in your office as a part of the premarital counseling sessions. Most people can fill out Form X in about an hour; but women usually take a little longer than men to complete it. You will find that you can score it in ten to fifteen minutes. But it usually takes at least an hour to go over it with each person. More time is required if there is very much discussion.

Since the decision to use the SKI may not be made until the private appointments, it may be difficult to schedule it. In most instances, however, the man and the woman may come to the office together for their individual interviews. While one is seeing you, the other may be taking the SKI. Similar to the procedure for using the premarital questionnaire, you need time to review both inventories before discussing them with either person. Again, this material will be confidential. But it is important for you to know the needs of each person before trying to guide one of them in being understanding and helpful to the partner.

As she approached her second marriage, a woman in her late twenties needed a great deal of help in the area of sex. Before her divorce two years before, she had been married for six years, and had had one child. One of the main reasons she had divorced her husband was sexual abuse. This was confirmed by her physician. She said she had not experienced an orgasm since the child was born, less than two years after their marriage, and no more than three or four times during those first two years. Even though she said she knew that sex was supposed to be a satisfying experience for women as well as men, the way she had been treated by her husband had so conditioned her against sex that she wondered if she could ever enjoy it, even with her new husband, who was a very gentle and considerate person.

Fortunately, the couple came for premarital counseling three months before the wedding, largely because the woman knew she had a sex problem and had discussed it with her partner. In addition to the two joint interviews and the two individual sessions, her premarital counseling included the SKI and six additional sessions, primarily on sexual attitudes and practices.

Even though the man indicated no special needs in the sex area, he also took the SKI and had three additional individual appointments. He did this in order to be able to understand what his future wife was experiencing and to learn how to be more helpful to her. Happily, within two months after marriage they reported some progress toward a mutually satisfying sexual experience.

How do you decide whether to give the SKI? Of course you will have to sense the need of each person as you discuss sex. In addition you can get some guidance from the way the person answers the sex-related questions on the premarital question-naire. Generally, if any three of the questions get negative responses, this alerts you to discuss with the person the possibility of taking the SKI.

Several examples may clarify what we mean. If a person has done little or no reading, has had little or no help from parents, and has a mother or father whose attitude toward sex is only "tolerating" or "rejecting," then that person may need the SKI. The same is true of persons who do not know how their parents feel about sex, and who had "mixed feelings" themselves. Also, anyone who asks for additional help in as many as three areas on question 34 may indicate that the SKI should be suggested. Certainly one who anticipates sexual relations either with "mixed feelings," or "somewhat fearfully," needs it. Or those who consider their present knowledge of sex inadequate, or who are doubtful about it should be apprised of the SKI possibility. A majority of men request "help for partner" on question 34, but of course this should be checked out with the woman herself. Some may need information but will not accept it. Our suggestion is that you offer as much help as is acceptable, but no more.

Review Visit to Physician

As a part of the discussion of sex you can inquire about the visit to the medical doctor. This may be done in such a way as to make it easy for the person to bring up any questions in this area that were not discussed with the doctor. A well-qualified physician may have completed a full health examination for both persons, as well as a vaginal examination for the woman, and given the couple a good report. The doctor may have prescribed a contraceptive, perhaps the Pill, but may not have taken time to discuss such matters as facilitating first intercourse, the importance of the excitement phase, the timing of penetration, positions, or frequency. If this is the case, you may need to do some of this. Or you may indicate where supplemental help is available in reading resources. You may also be able to help a couple to internalize information given by the physician.

You, of course, recognize that most physicians—even those qualified to do the premarital consultation—are so busy these days that they do not always take time to answer a couple's questions sufficiently. (We hope that pastors do take the time needed!) Or, knowing how busy the medical doctor is, a couple may hesitate to take the time they need. Frequently they have some questions about sex for their pastor that they did not ask their doctor. These questions may be in the area of attitudes and morals. Some couples, for example, still wonder what their church's policy is on birth control. Or they may ask for further information or guidance in sexual adjustment as indicated above.

You can also inquire about any reading that you suggested in the first interview. This can serve several purposes. One is to help the individual actually assimilate and utilize the information. Another is to emphasize the value of the reading and to encourage further reading as needed. Of course, this inquiry about reading should include any area of background or relationship the individual is interested in, and not be confined to sex. Occasionally couples will request additional recommendations of reading material.

But what if the review of the above items in-cluding the premarital questionnaire, does not produce any significant discussion? One possibility is to adjourn the session before the hour is up. However, if this is done, something significant might be overlooked.

Imagine Disagreement

A case in point is the rather mature couple in their middle twenties, who showed no disagreement in any area on their premarital questionnaires. The pastor thought them a rare couple indeed!

In his private appointment with the man the pastor said, "You indicate that you have had no disagreements, and that you do not expect to have any serious ones after you are married. What I want to ask you is this: If you could imagine yourselves having even a minor disagreement over something, what do you think it might be about?"

The young man thought a moment, mustered his courage, and replied, "She might be too bossy." The pastor invited him to explain what he meant. Gradually he opened up and reviewed some facts about his fiancée's family. Her father had died four years ago, but his insurance and her part-time work made it possible for her to finish college. Her mother had been an invalid for several years. He was proud of the fact that she had actually supported her family since she had graduated three years before. And, when married, they would continue to contribute to the support of her mother and her younger brother.

It was more difficult for him to explain that his fiancée had a little brother twelve years old. Because of the family situation she had been like a father and mother to the boy. Then the man came to the point as he said with deep feeling, "I guess I'm afraid she might treat me like her little brother." He sighed as though he was glad he had finally said it. "Yes, I'm afraid she might be too bossy."

The pastor explored these feelings with him. After extended conversation he finally reported, as if a light had come on, "You know, Pastor, I guess one of the main reasons I'm marrying her is that she's such a good manager." Then he added with a sly smile, "But she'd better not treat me like a little brother!"

In their fifth interview, almost six months after the wedding, this young man was almost exuberant as he remembered how the earlier premarital discussion had given him enough courage to talk with his wife about his fear of her bossiness and his appreciation of her managerial abilities. He felt that being able to talk about it together kept it from becoming a problem between them. If they had not brought it up, he felt he would always have been sensitive to any hint of control from her and would have found some way to strike back.

The pastor later reported that he believed this was one concern that never would have been brought up in a counseling session with both persons present. He believed it took the safety and the comfort of the private session to free the young man to discuss his problem.

Sometime before the end of the private appointment, you need to decide whether to recommend one or more *additional counseling sessions*. Of course you will evaluate this recommendation with the person involved. It may be rejected, but remember that you are responsible for taking the initiative in suggesting further counseling. Whenever the need becomes evident and time is available, the appointments should be scheduled as soon as possible, for additional counseling may reveal the need for other help.

Similarly, in the private appointment, you may discover that one or both of the partners needs to be referred to another professional person or agency. In such a case, we hope you will follow the best referral procedures.

In the next chapter we return to seeing the couple together.

In the fourth interview the couple are together again. For most couples, this session comes only one or two weeks before the wedding, so it is an opportunity for a last minute check-up. Also, for most couples, this will be only one session. But for others, if they begin early enough to allow time for it, and if you have time available, this "fourth interview" might be extended into several sessions, depending, of course, on the needs and wishes of the couple.

Again the idea is having enough flexibility of structure to meet people's needs and not simply to fill out a prescribed pattern of sessions. If this joint interview should develop into several sessions and take place in several steps, what is described here may occur in the last stages of these sessions. At this time the emphasis is not so much on needs and problems—although there may be some—but on positive plans for the couple's future together.

Purposes and Procedures

Basically, three purposes are to be achieved in this fourth interview. In addition, some of the tasks of the earlier interviews not yet completed may be carried over into this session. But mainly this is a time to look to the future and to close the pre-wedding sessions.

1. This is an opportunity to bring the two persons together again to make plans as a couple for their forthcoming marriage.

The private appointments, just concluded, focused on the individual's feelings about himself or herself as a marriage partner, about the future partner, and on his or her views of marriage. In many cases, these interviews may have concentrated largely on problems and tensions, with only minor attention given to the couple's strong points and to their planning together. This fourth session is the time to stress their strengths and to enhance their potential for growth together. This is the time for a positive emphasis on their future together.

2. As much as possible, this is also the time to help a couple complete the tasks of premarital counseling together. This purpose may be accomplished, more specifically, in five ways:

a. The two persons may continue to review critically their readiness for marriage, but emphasize now their ability to move ahead together. In a very few instances there will be exceptions, for some couples may find that this session is the time for a decision not to get married or to postpone marriage. If not done before, you can now finalize your own decision about whether or not you will marry the couple.

b. This is the time to help them summarize what they have learned from earlier attempts to identify and assess their needs, stressing now their strengths and inner resources.

c. As they face the future, you can help them discover resources available in the church and community that could enrich their marriage, both by what they receive and by what they give in serving others.

d. You can continue to help them make plans for their life together. You could do this by reviewing some, or all, of the developmental tasks, or by concentrating on a few specific areas of adjustment, such as money, planning for children, and religion.

e. You can also help the couple continue their efforts to solve problems. These may be problems that have not been faced previously, or that are yet to be worked out. But, with a look to the future, you can help the couple to be realistic in expecting to continue to have problems after they are married, and point out resources for handling such problems. You can do this so that they will not feel their marriage has failed the first time they have an argument.

3. A final purpose of this fourth session is to make a tentative closing of the pre-wedding counseling. The word *tentative* is used deliberately. Only the pre-marriage phase of premarital counseling ends with this session. The pattern here recommended includes a fifth interview to be scheduled from one to six months after the wedding. This plan is a definite effort to keep the counseling relationship open so that the couple will find it easy to return for continued counseling whenever they wish. Therefore, some specific reference should be made to the fifth interview, and directions should be given as to how they can make the contact.

Counseling After the Wedding

In some special situations most of the "premarital" counseling can be done after the wedding. Some couples may notify the pastor of their wedding plans too late to allow for more than one joint session beforehand. After the wedding, it may be appropriate to have one or more of both the individual and the joint sessions. These may be patterned very much like the premarital sessions. But, of course, they will deal with the "here and now" of their relationships.

Some pastors feel this kind of preventive counseling is actually superior to the pre-marriage sessions because they can deal with the couple's current relationship. Too much should not be expected, though, in situations where couples are simply not interested in counseling. You may find this is the reason why many do not notify you of their wedding plans early enough to permit premarital counseling. Very few of these uninterested persons follow through with counseling even after the sessions have been set up.

Technically, premarital counseling in the pre-wedding sessions closes with the fourth interview. But the overarching pastoral care relationship continues. It is appropriate, therefore, that you let the couple know of your continuing interest in them and their marriage. Some reference may be made to your looking forward to seeing them in the congregation and at other appropriate church or community meetings in which they may be involved.

As a part of your concern for the couple, we hope you will see that they are helped to join special couples' groups or classes in the church. Many of them—especially younger couples—are hesitant and may find it difficult to make the transition from a single to a married group. Needless to say, this is an opportunity for ministry on the part of couples who are already in such groups to reach out to the newlyweds.

Some pastors make it a practice to remember all couples on their wedding anniversaries in some special way. This may be done by sending them a greeting card or by writing a personal letter. This is one way to keep the possibility of counseling open, not by extending a direct invitation to them to come in but by communicating a continuing concern for their marriage. This practice could have real value for members of your congregation (but questionable value for couples who are members elsewhere).

Perhaps another word of caution should be given here to discourage you from any efforts to make couples dependent on you. We urge you to develop appropriate forms of ministry that will help couples in continuing to mature as autonomous responsible persons.

Procedures

There are several ways that the purposes of this interview can be achieved. First, it may be best to review certain questions from the premarital questionnaire and any concerns that have come up in the individual interviews that need the attention of both partners. Also, the couples may need to face some specific questions together, which may not have come up before, such as questions about budget, planning for children, or religious life. Third, they may summarize some of their learnings from the counseling sessions, which, we hope, will furnish encouraging guidelines for the future. Finally, any outstanding housekeeping details should be checked.

Reviewing the Premarital Questionnaires and reviewing specific problems from the individual interviews will vary, of course, with each couple. But certain questions may be anticipated and planned for after careful study of the forms. These should include any questions on which you believe additional work is indicated.

Some of this additional work might be done during the premarital sessions, when you can help the couple work through the issues. However, the couple will have to do much of the work after marriage. In this case you can call attention to possible problem areas. You can also make helpful suggestions about how growth and development could be facilitated. Often it will help if you simply alert couples to the fact that tensions may be expected in certain areas. Being so alerted is a kind of preparation for the experience itself. They are not taken by surprise, but are better able to proceed cooperatively with constructive action.

Additional work may be needed also when there are marked differences in *background*. The questionnaire contains several possibilities of this type. For instance, age may be an area of concern if the couple is very young, if they are old enough to be "set in their ways," or if there is a wide difference in age.

Depending on the section of the country and the particular community the couple live in, race or nationality could be an issue—especially if the partners' backgrounds are different. A great deal of give-and-take might be required if there is much difference in their religious, educational, or economic backgrounds. This might be true also if one person is an only child and the other one comes from a large family.

In the area of *relationships* there are many possibilities for further work. Four of these can be given special attention. The first is parental approval of the marriage. If this is a problem area, it probably would have come out in one of the earlier sessions. But now it may need to be faced by both persons together. Even when there is no disapproval, many young couples may still need help in realizing that they are establishing a new family, and that their primary loyalty now is to each other and not to their parents. It is very difficult for some persons to make this adjustment.

For couples marrying in the middle or older years, adjustments to other family members could center around their adult children, who might not approve of the marriage. In such cases, the children may be afraid the new mate will reduce their share of any inheritance that may be left.

The way a couple divide household responsibilities is another possible problem area. Each person's response on the questionnaire should be checked for agreement or disagreement on these role expectations and his or her intentions to perform household tasks. Again, something may have been said about this in the private appointments. But unless both the man and the woman have worked these through on their own, now is the time for them to get further help from joint counseling. Question 28 should also be related to question 7 regarding the experience and feelings of each partner about housework. You may be able to help couples find equitable ways of sharing household responsibilities, especially when both are employed full-time.

Another important area of adjustment is highlighted in question 29, regarding the partners' participation in certain *activities*, either together or separately. Perhaps more important is their feeling about the extent to which they share these activities. Certainly a couple must share enough common interests and activities from which to weave a relationship of durable quality.

Another crucial concern is the extent to which one person grants the other the freedom to be himself or herself. Some couples, therefore, will need guidance in cultivating common interests and growing in interpersonal competence. Others will need help in learning how to allow each other to develop individual interests. Ideally, marriage is a relationship of two equal persons, which strengthens and sustains each individual in developing creative selfhood.

Question 38 contains a number of possibilities for further work on *disagreements*. You may review with the couple the various items both of them checked in the first column indicating that they have no disagreement because the matter has "not arisen." Some items may need more attention.

One purpose of this review is to see what progress they have made between sessions in actually coming to grips with these disagreements. If they have not done their homework, you can draw them out and have them tell you the significance of some of their disagreements, and help them find ways they can face these disagreements in their future relationship. It should be helpful also to compare those items checked "none; not arisen" and "none; we agreed" with the checks in the last two columns on the page. Many of the items may have been discussed only superficially, and therefore may need further attention. This may be true also of some of the areas in which they indicate "little," "some," or "much" disagreement.

The most important thing in all of this, we think, is not to point out areas of disagreement. Rather, it is to assist the couple in finding ways of working out some of their disagreements and of coping with others. It is also helpful for them to realize the progress they have made.

The individual interviews may have revealed concerns that also need the attention of both persons in this fourth session. Perhaps, in the private conferences, you sensed this need and suggested that the individual initiate discussion of the subject with the partner. Or you may have encouraged the person to bring it up in the joint interview, if that seemed best.

If there is a crucial matter that needs attention, and neither of the above courses of action has been taken, what can you do? You could bring up the subject in a general way and encourage the couple to talk about it together.

Face Specific Questions

A second way to try to achieve the purposes of the fourth interview is to help the couple face some specific questions together that may not have come up earlier.

Developmental Tasks

One procedure is to go over each of the developmental tasks to find out what plans the couple have already made and what additional help can be given in this session. Since the various tasks will be discussed briefly in the next chapter, they are only listed here:[1]

1. Developing and sustaining a Christian way of life
2. Providing the necessities of life
3. Earning and spending
4. Establishing husband and wife roles
5. Creating and maintaining communication
6. Meeting personal and affectional needs
7. Planning for children
8. Adjusting to relatives
9. Making and keeping friends
10. Taking part in community life

This approach has two advantages. It provides a comprehensive coverage of the most important tasks the couple will face in marriage. It also focuses on the future, on what the couple will be trying to achieve together after they are married. Since a developmental task is something the couple must do themselves, you are limited in what you can do for them. But you can help them see the scope of their tasks in marriage, and can give them some guidelines for approaching these tasks.

Here is another alternative. Three specific items, if they have not been worked through satisfactorily earlier, ought to be worked on in this session. They are finances, planning for children, and religion (the comments given here supplement those made elsewhere in this manual and should be integrated with them).

Finances

In discussing finances, we think it is important for the couple to consider earning as well as spending. This includes the wife's working and all that this involves, as well as how her part of the income is to be used and how her working is related to planning for children.

The whole area of finances needs to be considered in the light of Christian principles of stewardship. In a world of limited resources, what are the implications for simplified living? Many persons make the mistake of assuming that if they have the money, it is all right to spend it.

This discussion should take into consideration the earlier comments about money, including the specific suggestions to be evaluated by the couple. In addition, the couple may want you to review their budget (see the couple's manual, chap. 7). In doing this, you should be sure they have not omitted some important items such as gifts, recreation, medical insurance, savings, and spending money.

Buying gifts for others can wreck a budget. Young couples especially are likely to have several friends getting married soon. And there is always the expense of birthdays and Christmas or other special occasions. Most couples make the mistake of thinking that they will not need very much money for recreation. They might think they can save money on dating as soon as they get married. You could ask them to budget for the kind of recreational and educational activities that they enjoy personally and that will strengthen their companionship.

A few couples may spend too much on insurance. However, most may not be aware of the importance of medical insurance, especially if they have not had to carry their own before. Rates of group insurance available through the business where they work or through professional organizations can be investigated and compared with individual policies.

Of course, it is possible to take all the joy out of living by overemphasizing savings. But most couples will need to be reminded of the importance of saving for emergencies. They may need to be encouraged to put aside from five to ten percent of their income as soon as they are able to do it. Another item often overlooked in budget making is allowances. Both partners should have some spending money that they do not have to account for to each other.

The budget can serve two purposes. First, it is a guide to spending, on which the couple have agreed in advance. Second, it provides a basis for reviewing spending at the end of the month and making whatever changes may be desirable or necessary.

Family Planning

Another specific item to be faced in the fourth interview by the couple together, if they have not done so before, is their planning for children. Be careful not to assume that all couples plan to have children. Today many couples are deciding not to become parents. The suggestions here are for couples who decide to have children. This subject is discussed briefly in the section on developmental tasks in the next chapter. Although a couple may not have their first child for perhaps two years, there are four sound reasons for discussing this concern in premarital counseling.

The first is to help the couple arrive at basic agreement on how many children they want to have and when, even though they may change their minds later. The second is to see that they have adequate medical advice for their family planning. Third, there may be several important factors to consider before making a decision to start their family, such as finances, both husband and wife working, further education, or living arrangements. Fourth, to get the subject out into the open, they need to talk about these considerations, although the actual decision may be many months in the making.

Checking both partners' responses to the Premarital Questionnaires might reveal that they already agree on whether they want to have children, or when and how many. If they did not agree, these questions might have already come up in the individual interviews. If not, the sooner agreement can be reached, the better. Question 35 should be checked with question 26 regarding the wife's working and how long she plans to work.

Some women plan to work "indefinitely," but want to have children in two years. They may have forgotten to consider the temporary or long-term loss of income, and will need to be guided in doing some careful financial planning to cover this period. Will the husband also take time off from work? Some women plan to work only until the first child is born and do not expect to return to work until the children are in school. This has implications regarding their plans for the use of the wife's income during these early years. If a high standard of living is established by living on two incomes, a necessarily lowered standard of living in the future may be blamed on the child, especially if there is an unplanned pregnancy.

Adequate medical advice regarding birth control is important to every couple, but more so to couples in special circumstances. They need to feel secure about the method of birth control they use, so that they can be free to enjoy sexual relations without any fear of an unplanned pregnancy. This is why it is important for you to find out how they feel about the advice and prescription they have received from their physician. This is especially true when couples have a special reason for waiting to have a child, such as the husband's need to complete his education and obtain a job with an adequate salary.

Some couples still have questions about the morality of contraceptives and may want to know their church's stand on birth control. It is not too early for a couple to begin to think about some of the factors involved in a decision about when to have their first child. Also, discussion of timing during the premarital counseling session can lessen the possibility of accidental parenthood.

Ideally, parenthood is seen as a Christian vocation. This means it is entered into in response to God's call to join in the creative process, both in bringing new life into the world, and in helping that child to grow to full maturity as a person in Christ. This means checking out such factors as the physical and emotional health of both parents, and especially the mother. It also means evaluating their educational and vocational plans, financial position, social conditions, and the needs of society, as well as their personal preferences. You can help the couple, however, to see the wisdom of not waiting too long to begin their family. If they wait for perfect conditions, they may never have any children. Most couples, however, understand that they need to allow themselves at least one or two years to adjust to each other before taking on the responsibility of parenthood.

Religion

The area of religious life, as already suggested, includes more than devotional life and church relationships, important as these are. We believe it is important to help a couple realize that their marriage relationship can be a channel for God's love, and that their marriage can be a means of service to the world.

You may inquire about the devotional life of each person and their plans for spiritual growth after marriage. You could encourage couples to have daily devotions together. You can do this by letting them know that you will give them a book of devotions for the first four weeks of marriage, possibly *Whom God Hath Joined* by David R. Mace. It is best to give them this book with the marriage certificate immediately after the wedding, so they can take it with them on the wedding trip. This book has so much helpful material that some pastors give it to all couples they marry, not just to those who expect to use it as a book of devotions.

In reviewing their church relationships you may ask how active each person is in the church and to what church each belongs. If there are differences indicated, these may have been faced earlier. But this is the time for the couple to plan for their future church life together. With your help, they may realize the significance of this aspect of their relationship. Unfortunately, at this stage in their life many couples do not see the value of church participation.

God's Love and Purpose

This counseling session is also an opportunity for you to help a couple rejoice in the fact that their relationship can express God's love. God is love and the source of their love for each other. God's love is unconditional—sacrificing, forgiving, sustaining, affirming.

Most important, however, is helping a couple realize that God has a purpose for their marriage—that their marriage is a means of service to others. The purposes of marriage include the ministry of husband and wife to each other and to their children. The purposes of marriage also extend beyond this to fulfilling God's will for them in the world today.

One way to open up this subject is to review responses to some of the items in question 38 of the premarital questionnaires—religion, values and life goals, political and social issues, and perhaps community activities. Another way to stimulate thought is to ask a couple what they hope to have accomplished in ten, twenty, or thirty years. What are they giving their lives to? For most couples, this could be an entirely new thought, and they might not know how to respond. But discussing their values and goals in life may help them begin to think about their marriage as a part of God's kingdom.

Summarize Learnings

In summarizing some of their learnings, it is good to let a couple point out some of the main areas in which they recognize that additional work is to be done, and to go over some of the ways they expect to continue working on these areas after marriage. Some of these may be differences or circumstances that they must find ways of coping with, and accept as givens. Others may be disagreements or problems that they feel they can work out with more time and

effort. Perhaps they have developed some skills in problem-solving that should be undergirded.

Not to be overlooked in this summary is a review of the strengths the couple have discovered or demonstrated. We think it is good to ask them to list these in specific terms. You can help them appreciate the value of these strengths in making their adjustments in marriage. Feel free to call their attention to any problems or strengths that they may have overlooked.

Be sure to guide them in utilizing appropriate resources in the church and community. If you feel good about the way these two persons have grown during the counseling sessions, be sure to say so. Do not hesitate to express positive evaluation whenever appropriate. A couple may have begun with several areas of tension or disagreement. In counseling they may have made considerable progress toward resolving some of them. Such positive experiences should be noted, and continued improvement encouraged.

In this summary emphasize the crucial significance of communication in marriage, if sufficient attention has not been given to this subject before. If this is the case, more extended discussion is called for. At the least remind the couple of some of the important elements of communication.[2] Reference can be made also to some specific suggestions on how to face disagreements, such as guides on "how to fight fair":[3]

> State exactly what you don't like, and how you want things changed.
> Focus on the issue, especially your feelings about it.
> Keep at it until you work things out.
> Decide on a simple next step for improvement.
> Get out the hurt; don't let it fester.
> Attack the problem; not one another.
> Don't drag in your relatives; keep them out.
> Let your partner know as your tension eases off.

To be sure, admonitions usually do not effect many changes, but some couples may appreciate being reminded that a good marriage requires effort, that they need to be careful not to take each other for granted, and that their marriage is worth working on together. They may also appreciate some guidance in how they can continue to grow in their relationship and find mutual fulfillment. Encourage them to keep their love growing through participating in marital growth activities, such as the Marriage Communication Lab, the Marriage Enrichment Retreat, or the Marital Support Group, referred to in chapter 4.

Housekeeping Details

Some "housekeeping" details might need attention during this interview. These may be details regarding books, the marriage license, the rehearsal, the wedding, or pastoral services.

1. *Books.* No doubt you will want each couple to keep *Preparing for Christian Marriage.* You may want to write a brief message of best wishes to them on the first page. Most books borrowed for special reading should be returned whenever the couple finishes them or perhaps by the time of the rehearsal. (Some pastors prefer to make gifts of one or more books. In some instances these are paid for by the church.) We think it is usually best for the couple to keep the books on sex and devotions until a month or so after the wedding.

If you use a book like *Your First Year of Marriage* by Tom McGinnis, you can encourage the couple to keep it longer or until the fifth interview. Or perhaps you will want to lend this book to the couple at the time of the fifth interview. Sometimes a couple find one or more of these books so helpful that they want to keep them for further reference or to share with their friends. If so, you can suggest that they purchase the books. You will find it necessary to keep records on your books, or you will lose many of them. You are apt to find it necessary to follow up on at least half of them.

2. *Marriage license.* A good practice is to have the couple bring their marriage license to you before the wedding, at least no later than the rehearsal. This could save an embarrassing delay of the wedding, since most states require you to have the license in hand before you perform the ceremony.

3. *Rehearsal.* You can help the couple anticipate the rehearsal as preparation for the worship service that the wedding will be, and you can conduct the rehearsal accordingly. If the bride plans to have someone stand in for her at the rehearsal, as some do, we urge you to find a time when you can help her walk through the service of holding hands and exchanging rings as the couple will do.

4. *Wedding.* Because of the excitement and strain the couple will experience during the wedding, we urge you to do all you can to reassure them that they need not worry about the details. You can explain that you will guide them through each step of the ceremony. This kind of reassurance and attention to detail can give confidence and ease to the couple.

And it can help them to be more aware of the meaning of the vows during the service itself.

5. *Pastoral services.* Before closing this interview, you may check on some pastoral services that you might render the couple. For example, if they are moving to another community, you may be able to help them establish a relationship to a new church or to groups or persons in the new community. If they are going to college, you will want to find out how to keep in touch with them, as well as how to help them become related to a religious group for married students on the campus.

6. *Plan for fifth interview.* Plans should be made to schedule the fifth interview from one to six months after the wedding. Be sure to make it clear that you are leaving the responsibility with the couple for initiating the contact. Help them feel free to call you at any time they wish. This fifth interview should be offered and anticipated, but the couple should not be coerced into accepting it.

It will be helpful to explain the nature of such an appointment. Most likely, it will be a review of the progress they are making in their adjustments with each other, and very similar to the pre-wedding sessions. Or, if appropriate, they may choose to use the time to work on one or more problem areas. When they want help with a particular problem, they should be encouraged to call you immediately. It is very important, as mentioned previously, that this be done in such a manner that dependence on you is not encouraged.

Prayer

Whether or not you have used prayer in previous sessions, you might want to close this final counseling session with a prayer of blessing on the couple and on their love and life together. You can actually pray the prayer for the couple in the ritual, instead of reading it. This could be the only time they will actually hear it, for they may be too excited at the wedding!

Generally, however, we believe it is best not to begin an appointment with prayer. This focuses attention on God, and you may not be sure what the person's attitude toward God is. Some persons may see God as a stern judge, who is condemning them for something they have done. This image makes them hesitate to bring up certain negative acts or feelings that should be discussed. We think it is better to let God's love be felt through your presence and caring for the couple.

When prayer is used at the end of a counseling

session, you will want to try to reflect whatever struggles or achievements have been discussed, or whatever resolutions have been made. Obviously, prayer is not to be used as a means of talking a person into something, or for trying to use God to get a person to come around to your point of view, however subtly this may be done.

In the next and last chapter we give some suggestions on how to conduct the fifth interview.

The fifth interview takes place from one to six months after the wedding. Actually this is an optional interview, and some couples will choose not to come for it. Nevertheless, the possibilities it offers for real help indicate that it should be suggested for all couples.

Major Purpose and Procedure

The major purpose of this fifth session is to keep the counseling relationship open, and to make it easy for the couple to return to counseling if they need and want it. If a problem comes up that calls for counseling, they do not have to hesitate to contact you. They already know that the interview is open for them.

For example, when a problem arises, one partner may say to the other, "The pastor is expecting us. Don't you think it's about time we called for that appointment?" The way is open to them to get help before a problem becomes too serious.

Availability is more a matter of attitude than schedule. Of course it is necessary for a couple to feel that you really care about them and their marriage—that you really want to help them. They also need to know that you have some ability to help them work out their problems. Then, given this attitude, the expectation of an interview facilitates their acceptance of available help.

Why is this fifth session set for one to six months after the wedding? One reason is to leave the date flexible so that the couple can schedule the appointment when they feel it will do them the most good. Enough time is thus allowed for them to work on some adjustments on their own; to settle down with each other, as it were. They know that help is available, but only if they need it.

The limit of six months is deliberately chosen. These first few months of marriage are crucial.[1] It is the time when two persons who are very different are trying to learn to adjust to each other in the most intimate relationship of life. Even couples who have been living together will be adjusting to a new state in life.

Generally more differences are evident during this time than at any other period of their marriage. They have less experience in making adjustments and in handling disagreements than at any later time. Consequently, this is the time when they are most likely to need help. They are not yet set in their ways, or resigned to living with their problems without doing something about them. They are apt to be eager to improve their marriage.

These first few months are also the time when the couple is setting patterns of adjustment that are likely to remain with them the rest of their lives. If the proper help is given as needed, they may be able to discover creative and satisfying ways of relating to each other.

Our experience is that only about one in four couples takes advantage of the opportunity for further counseling. We believe this is a significant number that makes the plan worth suggesting to all those who receive premarital counseling.

We also found that only about half of the couples in premarital counseling returned the books we lent them without some additional follow-up. Books are usually returned with a brief note of appreciation for the counseling and perhaps the message that the newlyweds are doing fine and do not need to see us. The other couples need to be reminded to return the books. You may write a reminder letter, and use the opportunity to add a paragraph about the suggested counseling session. You may remind them that they may call for an appointment at any time. But be sure to leave the decision to them, without making them feel guilty if they do not make an appointment.

With a few couples you may take the initiative in reminding them that you are looking forward to seeing them. You may suggest that they call you within a certain period of time, perhaps within a few days. However, when they do call, you should exert no pressure to get them to come in if they do not want counseling at this time. During the conversation, you can suggest a book, or indicate that you have one to lend them when you see them.

Procedure

Perhaps you are wondering how to conduct the fifth interview. Is it different from the other sessions? The two approaches of premarital counseling are still appropriate—educative and problem-solving.

Technically, however, the fifth interview is not premarital counseling. It is marriage counseling,[2] and it should be conducted as such when a couple take the initiative in seeking counseling and come with a problem they are ready to work on.

A very good questionnaire to use here is the Marital Adjustment Schedule 1A.[3] It should be filled out by each of the partners separately. You may use it very much as you do the premarital questionnaires.

Another resource to guide this interview is *A Marriage Role Expectation Inventory* by Marie S. Dunn, already referred to.[4] It can be used to encourage discussion on any important roles that emerge, very much as suggested in the earlier interview before marriage.

After marriage, a stimulating variation on this inventory may be used. On his form, the husband rates each role according to the way he sees himself *actually performing* the role at the present time. Simultaneously, the wife rates another copy of the husband's form according to the way she *would like* him to perform each role. The same procedure is followed in rating two sets of the wife's inventory by both partners. This process allows for the comparison of *role performance* and *role expectation*, which can be a very healthy exercise.

When couples come in primarily to complete the premarital arrangement for the fifth interview, you can review their premarital counseling records as a part of your preparation for the session. You may find several concerns or areas that seemed very significant at the time and that you noted for follow-up in this fifth session.

Developmental Tasks

Another approach is to review the couple's growing relationship on the basis of developmental tasks.[5] This is a very comprehensive approach. It is all-inclusive and allows for a rather full examination of the various areas of adjustment, including husband and wife roles. However, it does require more skill and much more time than the others suggested.

This approach gives the couple an opportunity to evaluate their success, so far, in marriage. It also gives you a framework within which you can structure the content of the interview. You can then adapt any structure or content to the needs of the couple and to the time available for counseling.

The developmental-task approach has some distinctive features. It includes certain areas of adjustment and fits them into a pattern of overall development. Instead of considering one area of adjustment as though it were a separate part of a couple's relationship, as the earlier-mentioned subject method is likely to do, the developmental approach emphasizes the interrelatedness of the various tasks.

The tasks arise from three roots. These are primarily the total-person maturation (physical, emotional, social, and so forth) of the husband and wife, the cultural expectations regarding married couples, and the values and goals of the couple. The developmental tasks are seen as "inner" responsibilities of the couple—no one else can accomplish the tasks for them—and also as foundations for later development. This approach views marriage as a comprehensive, developmental, dynamic growth process, not as a once-for-all, static achievement.

For a comprehensive coverage, ten developmental tasks should be explored with each couple. You should not try to impose your interpretation of these tasks on the couple. Nevertheless, as a minister of the gospel, you will take the responsibility for helping them see the value of the Christian faith in each task they face. These are the ten developmental tasks.[6]

1. *Developing and sustaining a Christian style of life.* This task includes working out a common philosophy of life, a moral and spiritual value system, and personal motivation for living. All of these are expressed in their style of life. The task involves agreeing on religious practices in the home and participation in the life and work of the church. Such religious commitment calls for the intermeshing of two formerly differing ways of life. This can be very difficult for some, especially if a husband and wife come from different religious backgrounds. It may be difficult also if one has been accustomed to

being more active in church than the other. One of the partners may have no religious inclination at all.

Establishing a common religious philosophy and practice is perhaps both the most difficult and the most important task a couple has; one that may take a long time and may never be fully achieved. For life is ever-changing and faith is ever-growing. But you can help them to see that this task is worth working at; for it is the foundation of their life together, and it determines the way they work at all the other developmental tasks. You can also help them to evaluate the way their Christian style of life is expressed in the other tasks.

2. *Providing the necessities of life.* The emphasis here is usually on finding and maintaining a place to live. This may be a small one-room rented apartment or a large, fully furnished house. A couple's task will be to make it *home* for them. Finding and furnishing the new residence demands many immediate decisions on a joint basis, very different from their previous decision-making. Compromise is often necessary— perhaps in the location of the house and in taste in furnishings. One or both of the partners may have to be satisfied with less than they were accustomed to in their parental home.

The necessities of life also include such items as food, clothing, medical care, and transportation. Providing these, too, will call for many joint decisions and adjustments, even though some individual tastes may be respected. The main thing is for the couple actually to experience working together as a team in handling these choices and in getting settled in a home base together. You can help couples, not only to be considerate of each other in making their decisions, but also to evaluate their decisions in the light of their values and goals in life.

3. *Earning and spending income.* The couple will want to develop mutually acceptable methods of earning and spending their money, and ways of managing and using any possessions or other resources they may have. Marriage may necessitate a change in jobs for one or both partners.

A major item for consideration here may be whether the wife will work—which is more and more the rule these days. When both husband and wife work, it may be necessary to make adjustments in schedules, transportation, and household tasks. What are their feelings, for example, about adjustments that may be required if the wife's work means their moving to another city, or if her income is larger than his? The feelings about and meanings of their adjustments ought to be worked through fully.

Again, values and goals play a vital role in spending as well as in earning money. We hope these values and goals will guide the couple in their whole lifestyle, as well as in deciding just what amounts they allow in their budget for each item. A budget, or some form of spending plan, should be mutually agreed upon. You can help them see the importance of decisions' now being made together, rather than independently. Marriage also requires more thought for the future, perhaps in the form of savings and insurance. The important question here is this: Does the couple become a partnership in arriving at a mutually satisfying earning and spending plan?

4. *Establishing husband and wife roles.* Couples have decisions to make about who does what and who is responsible to whom. Today couples have more freedom in managing their affairs. In the past, husband and wife roles were more clearly defined. For many couples the husband was to be the "head of the house," the one in authority. The wife stayed at home and carried the household responsibilities, while the husband went out and worked at his job. With the present-day emphasis on equality between the sexes, and with so many wives working outside the home, the old, clearcut patterns are changing.

For many couples, these changing patterns are creating confusion, and even conflict. Their attitudes and feelings about the changing roles are more important than what they actually do. A husband may feel he has failed as a breadwinner if his wife works, especially if he grew up in a home where his mother never worked outside the home and his parents placed a high value on the husband's role of supporting the family. Frequently, negative feelings—such as a husband's feelings of inadequacy— are not brought out into the open. You can help them deal with these feelings.

We believe that decisions regarding roles should be made by the couple together, taking their feelings into account, and considering the wisdom of change. Otherwise, decisions may be made by default and create an underlying tension. Couples may need help in learning to be sensitive to each other's personal preferences and abilities as they work out their responsibilities together.

5. *Creating and maintaining communication.* Couples need to find meaningful ways of communicating with each other, emotionally and intellectually. This means creating a system of give-and-take, not one partner's simply telling the other something.

Learning to be sensitive to each other's feelings is far more important than just hearing the words that are said. Meaning is most likely to be in the feelings.

This deeper meaning can be communicated in actions more than in words. Not that words are unimportant, however, for some words carry a great deal of freight.

Each partner needs to learn not only how to "get the message," but also how to be willing and able to make an appropriate response. In fact, the best kind of communication is that which occurs when one partner is so sensitive to the other's need that the response comes before the other has asked.

Establishing lines of communication also means finding ways of handling disagreements or conflicts. Some couples think they are protecting their relationship by overlooking differences. Just the opposite is apt to be true. Instead of protecting their relationship, they may be making it more superficial and perhaps more fragile. Facing differences and working them through on a problem-solving basis in most cases actually strengthens the relationship and deepens intimacy.

Some couples may need your help in learning how to make decisions together, or how to reopen lines of communication once they have been disrupted.

6. *Meeting personal and affectional needs.* One of the most important developmental tasks in the beginning of marriage is the couple's establishing mutually satisfying ways of meeting their personal and affectional needs.

By personal needs, we mean the whole area of an individual's psychological or emotional needs that requires attention and nourishment from the partner. For example, a person may need to be affirmed as a separate individual, as a person of worth, and may need to have a sense of self-esteem fed and strengthened in healthy ways. The need for respect and privacy is part of this total need.

By affectional needs, we mean the couple's need for sharing, for mutual give-and-take, and for fellowship and companionship. One part of this is their need for finding fulfillment with each other in their sexual relations (though not in this area alone).

Couples may need help in understanding that neither the personal nor the affectional needs should be minimized, for both are essential. This calls for a sensitive appreciation of the sometimes ambivalent needs for intimacy and distance, for companionship and privacy, for a sense of belonging and sturdy individuality. And all of these needs are so intertwined that they can be separated only for purposes of examination and evaluation. These needs should be seen as related to interests and activities, some shared and some private, as well as to the whole matter of personality adjustment.

7. *Planning for children.* Another task for couples is to decide whether they want to have children or not. If they do, they need to agree on plans for having children. This means talking together about how many children they would like to have, how soon, and their spacing. Timing is necessarily related to the wife's working. Some couples are deciding not to have children and more couples are deciding to have fewer children, perhaps only one or two.

Today as a total group, more and more couples are having their children earlier after marriage (eighteen months to two years) and closer together in age (about two years apart). However, a few couples (especially if the wife wants to establish her career or a couple wants to travel, and so forth) are delaying having their first child for several years. Most couples find it best to give themselves enough time to get adjusted to each other before they take on the responsibility of adjusting to a child.

Our church believes that every child should be wanted and planned for as a gift from God. Therefore, it approves of planned parenthood, and urges couples to get the best medical advice available and find the method best suited to their needs. An unplanned pregnancy can be a real crisis in the life of a couple, especially if they are still struggling to get started in life together. But if such a pregnancy does occur, they should know that their pastor is available to help them adjust to the new situation in the most constructive manner possible.

8. *Adjusting to relatives.* The task of adjusting as a married couple to relatives in the larger families of in-laws on both sides is a big one. The adjustment, however, usually centers around getting along with the parents.

Many couples feel that only the husband and the wife are getting married, and that they do not need to concern themselves with their immediate families, and especially not with more distant relatives. But actually, two whole families are coming into a new relationship through the marriage. The exact kind of relationship depends on just how close various family members are.

Some couples may have a struggle in establishing their independence from their parents. They may need your support in maintaining the primacy of their own marriage as a new unit and in being able to stand on their own feet. One or both persons may still be too dependent on the parents, or may feel guilty about moving out of the parental home, especially when some emotional or financial need is involved. However, the separation is necessary if the new marriage is to have a life of its own. This does not mean that couples need to cut themselves off from their parental families. But it does mean that they will have to find new ways of relating to relatives that will be satisfying.

9. *Making and keeping friends*. Newly married couples are faced with the task of making many adjustments with friends and associates. You can help them to be realistic in this task at four points.

First, some couples are unrealistic in thinking that they do not need any friends after they are married. They are so much in love and are finding all their interests so absorbing that they think they only need each other! Obviously, thinking that two people can meet all of each other's fellowship needs is expecting too much of them and of their marriage. It is all right for the couple to be alone for a time, but soon after the honeymoon it will be important for them to move out into social activities with others.

A second mistake some couples make is in thinking that friendships take care of themselves, that they need to do nothing to initiate or maintain them. Possibly many social activities involving friends did develop easily and naturally before marriage. But afterward, more deliberate effort seems to be required. It may be, too, that popular persons were on the receiving end of friendship before marriage. Marriage, however, changes all of this. For marriage has moved the couple into a different world, where responsibilities for entertaining are more equalized.

Third, a couple must decide which of their old friends they want to keep. Most couples come to marriage with three sets of friends—his, hers, and theirs. Each of the partners probably had some friends not very well known to the other partner. These friendships might create some tensions after marriage. One person might not like certain of the other's friends, but may not say much about it until after marriage. Maintaining friendships with members of the opposite sex, especially if they are still single, can also raise questions. Often a single person, male or female, is considered a threat by one's partner. It is good for both husband and wife to realize this and find some agreeable way of making decisions and maintaining the relationships both of them want to keep.

Fourth, there is the matter of making new friends. A couple needs to realize the value of new friends, and may need help in actually making contacts. Perhaps the new friends will also be newly married couples, but some may be of a different age group. In either case, friendships can be formed around interests and activities that the couples enjoy or in which they find meaning. You may be able to help

the new couple become related to a group in the church or community. Or if they are moving to a new community—as four out of five people do at the time of marriage, or within a year after marriage—you may be able to help them make contact with a congenial group by contacting the pastor of the church where they are going.

In addition, couples may find it necessary to adjust to certain business entertaining that is expected of them because of their jobs. Finding a workable plan for creating and sustaining friendships with business associates is also part of this ninth developmental task.

10. *Taking part in community life*. The final developmental task of newlyweds, and one that is often overlooked, is finding a place for themselves in various community activities, organizations, or movements. These include state, national, and world interests, even though the focus is often on their local community.

Many couples are unrealistic in thinking that they can withdraw from the world, and live in isolation from the social forces around them. They need help from their pastor in realizing that they are a part of their community and that they have an opportunity and responsibility to contribute to the shaping of the culture. Social forces impinge on their lives whether they choose to let this happen or not.

Many couples today have a very keen sense of social responsibility. But they may need help in making their influence effective. They might be very much opposed to many of the things happening in their community, nation, and world; but they might not be as certain about how they can work toward bettering conditions. Some become disillusioned very quickly. This could be partly because of the hypocrisy, and often outright dishonesty, they discover among organizations or people whom they have formerly respected. It could also be due to the fact that they are unrealistic in expecting reforms overnight. They need your encouragement and support; encouragement to take part in various organizations and movements that are at work for community betterment of one kind or another. They will surely need your support (and the support of whatever segments of the Christian community can be rallied) if they are not to be discouraged by the opposition they are certain to encounter.

Many couples really want to move into various community organizations and activities, but they do not know how to make the necessary contacts. This is more likely to be true if they are newcomers to the community, especially if it is a large urban area. You may have an opportunity to guide them to the proper contacts through various other members of the church—one advantage of counseling in the context of the Christian community. Joint participation in those aspects of community life on which both agree can strengthen their relationship. Their lives and influence can contribute much to the community.

Primarily, however, this developmental task, like all the others, is the responsibility of the couple. As their pastor, in counseling, you can alert them to the task and can stimulate them to work on it. You can encourage them in it, but the task is theirs.

In conclusion, the fifth interview may be a kind of health checkup that shows that everything is in good order. On the other hand, this review may reveal problem areas that require one or more additional sessions for extended counseling. The fifth interview could also be the time to encourage the couple for a marriage enrichment event as suggested in chapter 4.

Our hope is that, whatever approach you choose, your couples will find it helpful in solving problems and enriching their marriages. We also hope that you will find a sense of satisfaction in knowing that you have made a contribution to others as you share yourself and your abilities. We believe that God's love is available to each of us and can be transmitted to others in many ways. We think one of the most exciting ways can be our working to enrich and strengthen those who prepare for marriage.

CHAPTER 1

[1]Figures cited here and immediately following are from the study by Gerald Kingsbury Hill, "Premarital Counseling Practices and Attitudes Among Ministers of The Methodist Church" (doctoral dissertation, Teachers College, Columbia University, 1969), pp. 57-58. This is the most thorough study we know in the field. For more recent but less extensive studies see "Trends in Premarital Counseling" by Walter R. Schumm and Wallace Denton in *The Journal of Marital and Family Therapy*, October 1979, pp. 23-32, which also has an extensive bibliography.

[2]Aaron L. Rutledge, *Premarital Counseling* (Cambridge, Mass.: Schenkman Publishing Co., 1966), p. xiii; Richard A. Hunt and Edward J. Rydman, *Creative Marriage* (Boston: Holbrook Press, 1976), pp. 126-28; John L. C. Mitman, *Premarital Counseling* (New York: Seabury Press, 1980), pp. xii ff; Robert F. Stahmann and William J. Hiebert, *Premarital Counseling* (Lexington, Mass.: D. C. Heath, 1980), pp. 3 ff; and Ed Bader's report in *Family Therapy News*, vol. 12, no. 4, July, 1981 (AAMET, Upland, CA).

[3]Judson T. and Mary G. Landis, *Building a Successful Marriage* (New York: Prentice-Hall, 1968), pp. 112-14.

[4]For the family life cycle, see Leon Smith, *Family Ministry*, pp. 66-67, available from Discipleship Resources, P.O. Box 840, Nashville, Tenn. 37202. This cycle is adapted from Evelyn Millis Duvall, *Marriage and Family Development* (Philadelphia: J. B. Lippincott Co., 1977), pp. 137 ff.

[5]See Howard Clinebell, *Growth Counseling* (Nashville: Abingdon, 1979), chap. 6.

CHAPTER 2

[1]For fuller treatment, see Howard J. Clinebell, Jr., *Basic Types of Pastoral Counseling* (Nashville: Abingdon, 1966), pp. 41-56.

[2]Hill, "Premarital Counseling Practices," p. 56.

[3]Gerald Gurin et al. *Americans View Their Mental Health* (New York: Basic Books, 1960), p. 307.

[4]Charles Stewart, *The Minister As Family Counselor* (Nashville: Abingdon, 1979), pp. 168-72.

[5]For information, write Marriage Encounter, Inc., 955 Lake Drive, St. Paul, Minn. 55120.

[6]For information, contact your denominational headquarters, or write Marital Growth Programs, P.O. Box 840, Nashville, Tenn. 37202.

CHAPTER 3

[1]For another view, see Mitman, *Premarital Counseling*, pp. 1-19.

[2]For a particular explanation and application of these, see *The Book of Discipline of The United Methodist Church 1980*, pp. 78-81

CHAPTER 4

[1]For another sample copy, see Howard Clinebell's *Growth Counseling for Marriage Enrichment, Pre-Marriage and the Early Years* (Philadelphia: Fortress Press, 1975). For a different approach, see Stahmann and Hiebert, *Premarital Counseling*, chaps. 7 and 8.

[2]For recommended reading see page 85.

[3]For information on marriage enrichment retreats such as The United Methodist Church's Marriage Communication Labs and its Marriage Enrichment Weekends, contact Antoinette and Leon Smith (1605 Otter Creek Road, Nashville, Tenn. 37215). Another marriage enrichment model is described in Larry Hof's and William R. Miller's *Marriage Enrichment: Philosophy, Process and Program* (Bowie, Md.: Brady, 1981).

[4]For information on how to operate a marital growth group, write to ACME—Association of

Couples for Marriage Enrichment—P.O. Box 10596, Winston-Salem, NC 27108. We encourage you to join ACME and receive a bimonthly newsletter which contains suggestions for support groups. Or your groups may use the exercises described in David and Vera Mace's book *How to Have a Happy Marriage* (Nashville: Abingdon, 1977). This book is a step-by-step guide to an enriched relationship, which any couple can use entirely on their own.

[5]For a detailed description, see "Developing a National Marriage Communication Lab Training Program," by Antoinette and Leon Smith, in *Marriage and Family Enrichment: New Perspectives and Programs*, ed. Herbert A. Otto (Nashville: Abingdon, 1976).

[6]For the names and addresses of trained leader couples in your area, contact your denominational headquarters for the name and address of the chairperson (couple) of your marital growth program. Or write to the Marital Growth Programs, Board of Discipleship, P.O. Box 840, Nashville, TN 37202.

[7]For a schedule of training sessions or a list of trained leaders in your area, write to the Interpersonal Communication Programs, Inc., 1925 Nicollet Ave., Minneapolis, MN 55403. See *Alive and Aware* by Sherod Miller, Elan Munnally and Daniel Wackman (Interpersonal Communications Program, 1975). For a more popular treatment, see *Talking Together* (1979) by the same authors.

CHAPTER 5

[1]Charles William Stewart, *The Minister as Marriage Counselor* (Nashville: Abingdon, 1970).

[2]See Clinebell, *Growth Counseling*, chap. 6.

[3]For a good summary, see Gary F. Kelly, *Sexuality: The Human Perspective* (Woodbury, N.Y.: Barron's Educational Series, 1980), chap. 6. For more extensive treatment, see William Masters and Virginia Johnson, *Homosexuality in Perspective* (Boston: Little, Brown, 1979) and Allen Bell and Martin Weinberg, *Homosexualities* (New York: Simon & Schuster, 1978). For a counselor's views, see Clinton R. Jones, *Homosexuality and Counseling* (Philadelphia: Fortress Press, 1974) and *Understanding Gay Relatives and Friends* (New York: The Seabury Press, 1978), Leon Smith, ed., *Homosexuality: In Search of a Christian Understanding*, and "Homosexuality and Families— A Resource Packet for Families and Local Church Leaders" (3159C), available from Discipleship Resources, P.O. Box 840, Nashville, TN 37202, at $2.50.

[4]See Stewart, *Minister as Marriage Counselor*, pp. 55, 58, for a brief discussion of the use of tests; see also Stahmann and Hiebert, *Premarital Counseling*, chapter 9.

CHAPTER 6

[1]Nancy Friday, *My Mother/My Self* (New York: Dell Books, 1977), pp. 72-73.

[2]"Here is one of the 'teachable moments' or opportunities for learning, the like of which comes only a few times after early childhood. With the total impetus of nature, tremendous growth can occur, if motivation is stimulated and direction is provided. A minimum of concentrated help here can bring about personality changes which might take years of psychotherapy to effect later." Rutledge, *Pre-marital Counseling*, p. 7.

[3]See Stewart, *Minister as Marriage Counselor*, pp. 55-58, for a discussion of the use of tests. See also David Olson *et al.*, *Prepare II*, a scientifically developed program offering a diagnostic tool for professionals. Requires training for use. Contact Prepare, Inc., P.O. Box. 190, Minneapolis, MN 55440.

[4]See Hunt and Rydman, *Creative Marriage*, pp. 107 ff.

[5]Hill, "Premarital Counseling Practices," pp. 77-78.

[6]To help you integrate your sexuality and theology as a whole person and to be more comfortable with your own sexuality and able to discuss sex more freely, we urge you to take part in a Human Sexuality Forum or Sexual Attitude Reassessment Seminar. For events in your area, contact your denominational headquarters, or write to the National Sex Forum, 1523 Franklin St., San Francisco, Calif. 94109.

CHAPTER 7

[1]For this approach, see Clinebell, *Growth Counseling*.

[2]Resources recommended for physicians include a very detailed procedure (considered too much by some medical doctors) by Joseph B. Trainer, "Pre-Marital Counseling and Examination" in the *Journal of Marital and Family Therapy*, April, 1979, pp. 61-78. See also Rutledge, *Pre-marital Counseling*, especially chap. 8, "The Physician's Role in Preparation for Marriage"; Richard H. Klemer, *Counseling in Marital and Sexual Problems* (Baltimore: Williams & Wilkins Co., 1965); and Clark E. Vincent, *Human Sexuality in Medical Education and Practice* (Springfield, Ill.: Charles C. Thomas, Publisher, 1968).

[3]Mary S. Calderone, *Manual of Contraceptive Practice* (Baltimore: Williams & Wilkins Co., 1963), pp. 96-103, from a study of North Carolina reported by Ethel M. Nash.

[4]AAMFT headquarters are 924 W. Ninth St.,

Upland, CA 91786; AASECT headquarters are 600 Maryland Ave., SW, Washington, DC 20024.

[5]For help with the whole area of mixed marriage, see Albert I. Gordon, *Intermarriage: Interfaith, Interracial, Interethnic* (Boston: Beacon Press, 1964); Hunt and Rydman, *Creative Marriage*, pp. 286ff.; James L. McCary, *Freedom and Growth in Marriage* (Hamilton, 1975), pp. 337 ff.; Judson T. and Mary G. Landis, *Building a Successful Marriage*, chap. 13.

CHAPTER 8

[1]See Thomas Gordon, *Parent Effectiveness Training* (New York: Wyden Books, 1970); Miller, Nunally, and Wackman, *Alive and Aware*.

[2]For a good discussion of the process, see Tom McGinnis, *Your First Year of Marriage* (New York: Doubleday & Co., 1967), chap. 4. Also Duvall, *Marriage and Family Development*, p. 200.

CHAPTER 9

[1]Carl Rogers, *On Becoming a Person* (Boston: Houghton Mifflin, 1961), pp. 50-55. Copyright © 1961 Houghton Mifflin Company. Used by permission of Houghton Mifflin; and by permission of Constable and Co., London, Publishers in the British Commonwealth.

CHAPTER 10

[1]Adapted from Stewart, *The Minister as Marriage Counselor*, p. 21.

[2]See Clinebell, *Basic Types of Pastoral Counseling*, chap. 11. For other examples, see Mitman, *Premarital Counseling*, and Stahmann and Hiebert, *Premarital Counseling*.

[3]For an emphasis on the psychotherapeutic approach, see Rutledge, *Pre-marital Counseling*. Note, however, his recognition of the appropriateness of both types of counseling, pp. 58-63. For group counseling and couple counseling, see Robert F. Stahmann and William J. Hiebert, *Premarital Counseling*.

[4]See Clinebell, *Basic Types of Pastoral Counseling*, pp. 191-93.

CHAPTER 11

[1]See Stewart, *Minister as Family Counselor*.

CHAPTER 12

[1]See Smith, *Family Ministry*, chap. 9.

[2]This one and others are available from Family Life Publications, Inc., P.O. Box 427, Saluda, NC 28773.

CHAPTER 13

[1]See James A. Peterson, *Married Love in the Middle Years* (New York: Association Press, 1968) or Peterson and Payne, *Love in the Later Years* (New York: Association Press, 1975).

[2]Available with *Marriage Counselor's Manual and Teacher's Handbook* by Gelolo McHugh (1968), from Family Life Publications, P.O. Box 427, Saluda, NC 28773.

CHAPTER 14

[1]Adapted from Duvall, *Marriage and Family Development*, chap. 8.

[2]See "Learning to Speak the Same Language," pp. 29-49, and "Reaching Decisions and Settling Disagreements," pp. 55-83, in McGinnis, *Your First Year of Marriage*.

[3]See George Bach and Peter Wyden, *The Intimate Enemy* (New York: William Morrow & Co., 1969) and David and Vera Mace, *How to Have a Happy Marriage*, pp. 97ff.

CHAPTER 15

[1]This is the thesis of McGinnis in *Your First Year of Marriage*.

[2]There are a number of good books in this field, such as Stewart's *Minister as Marriage Counselor*.

[3]Available from the Marriage Council of Philadelphia, 4025 Chestnut Street, Philadelphia, PA 19104.

[4]Available from Family Life Publications, P.O. Box 427, Saluda, NC 28773.

[5]See Duvall, *Marriage and Family Development*, chap. 8.

[6]Duvall, *Marriage and Family Development*, lists eight tasks. We list ten here to emphasize Christian lifestyle, communication, and community relationships (see especially chap. 9, "Married Couples").

Bach, George and Peter Wyden. *The Intimate Enemy*. New York: William Morrow & Co, 1969.

Barbach, Lonnie. *For Yourself: The Fulfillment of Female Sexuality*. New York: Doubleday, 1975.

Bell, Allen, and Martin Weinberg. *Homosexualities*. New York: Simon & Schuster, 1978.

Bernard, Jessie. *The Future of Marriage*. New York: World Publishing Co., 1972.

Bright, Richard and Jean Stapleton. *Equal Marriage*. Nashville: Abingdon, 1977.

Calden, George. *I Count, You Count*. Niles, Ill.: Argus Communications, 1976.

Calderone, Mary S. *Manual of Contraceptive Practice*. Baltimore: Williams & Wilkins Co., 1963.

Calderone, Mary, ed. *Sexuality and Human Values*. New York: Association Press, 1974.

Chernick, Beryl and Noam. *In Touch*. New York: Macmillan, 1977.

Clinebell, Charlotte. *Counseling for Liberation*. Philadelphia: Fortress Press, 1976.

Clinebell, Charlotte and Howard. *The Intimate Marriage*. New York: Harper & Row, 1970.

Clinebell, Howard J. *Basic Types of Pastoral Counseling*. Nashville: Abingdon, 1966.

Clinebell, Howard. *Growth Counseling*. Nashville: Abingdon, 1979.

Clinebell, Howard. *Growth Counseling for Marriage Enrichment, Pre-Marriage and the Early Years*. Philadelphia: Fortress Press, 1975.

Clinebell, Howard. *Growth Groups*. Nashville: Abingdon, 1977.

Duvall, Evelyn Millis. *Marriage and Family Development*. Philadelphia: J. B. Lippincott Co., 1977.

Friday, Nancy. *My Mother/My Self*. New York: Dell Books, 1977.

Gordon, Albert I. *Intermarriage: Interfaith, Interracial, Interethnic*. Boston: Beacon Press, 1964.

Gordon, Thomas. *Parent Effectiveness Training*. New York: Wyden Books, 1970.

Gurin, Gerald et al. *Americans View Their Mental Health*. New York: Basic Books, 1960.

Hiebert, William J. *Klemer's Counseling in Marital and Sexual Problems*. Baltimore: Williams & Wilkins Co., 1977.

Hill, Gerald Kingsbury. "Premarital Counseling Practices and Attitudes Among Ministers of The Methodist Church." Doctoral dissertation, Teachers College, Columbia University, 1969.

Hof, Larry, and William R. Miller, *Marriage Enrichment: Philosophy, Process and Program*. Bowie, Md.: Brady, 1981.

Hunt, Richard A., and Edward J. Rydman, *Creative Marriage*. Boston: Holbrook Press, 1976.

Jones, Clinton R. *Homosexuality and Counseling*. Philadelphia: Fortress Press, 1974.

Jones, Clinton R. *Understanding Gay Relatives and Friends*. New York: The Seabury Press, 1978.

Kaplan, Helen Singer. *Disorders of Sexual Desire*. New York: Brunner/Mazel, 1979.

Kaplan, Helen Singer. *The New Sex Therapy*. New York: Brunner/Mazel, 1974.

Kelly, Gary F. *Sexuality: The Human Perspective*. Woodbury, N.Y.: Barron's Educational Series, 1980.

Kosnik, Anthony. *Human Sexuality: New Directions in American Catholic Thought*. New York: Paulist Press, 1977.

Landis, Judson T., *Marriage and Family Living*. New York: Prentice-Hall, 1975.

Landis, Judson T., and Mary G. *Building a Successful Marriage*. New York: Prentice-Hall, 1968.

Lasswell, Marcia and Norman Lobsenz. *No Fault Marriage*. New York: Ballantine Books, 1977.

Lederer, William and Don Jackson. *Mirages of Marriage*. New York: W. W. Norton & Co., 1968.

Leslie, Robert C. and Margaret G. Alter. *Sustaining Intimacy*. Nashville: Abingdon, 1978.

McCary, James L. *Freedom and Growth in Marriage*. Hamilton, 1975.

McCary, J. L. *Human Sexuality*. 2d ed. New York: Van Nostrand Reinhold Co., 1977.

Mace, David. *Getting Ready for Marriage*. Nashville: Abingdon, 1972.

Mace, David. *Marriage Enrichment in the Church*. Nashville: Broadman Press, 1977.

Mace, David and Vera. *How to Have a Happy Marriage*. Nashville: Abingdon, 1974.

Mace, David and Vera. *We Can Have Better Marriages*. Nashville: Abingdon, 1974.

McGinnis, Tom. *Your First Year of Marriage*. New York: Doubleday & Co., 1967.

McHugh, Gelolo. *Marriage Counselor's Manual and Teacher's Handbook*. Saluda, N.C: Family Life Publications, 1968.

Masters, William and Virginia Johnson. *Homosexuality in Perspective*. Boston: Little, Brown, 1979.

Masters, William and Virginia Johnson. *The Pleasure Bond*. Boston: Little, Brown, 1975.

Miller, Sherod, Elam Nunnally, and Daniel Wackman. *Alive and Aware*. Minneapolis: Interpersonal Communications Program, 1975.

Miller, Sherod, Elam Nunnally, and Daniel Wackman. *Talking Together*. Minneapolis: Interpersonal Communications Program, 1979.

Mitman, John L. C. *Premarital Counseling*. New York: Seabury Press, 1980.

Mollenkott, Virginia Ramey. *Women, Men and the Bible*. Nashville: Abingdon, 1977.

Nelson, James A. *Embodiment*. Minneapolis: Augsburg Publishing House, 1978.

Ogg, Elizabeth. *New Ways to Better Marriages*. Public Affairs Pamphlet 547, Public Affairs Committee, 381 Park Avenue, South, New York, NY 10016, 1977.

Oglesby, William B. *Referral in Pastoral Counseling*. New York: Prentice-Hall, 1968.

Olson, David, *et al. Prepare II. Minneapolis: Prepare Inc., 1979.*

Otto, Herbert A. *Marriage and Family Enrichment: New Perspectives and Programs*. Nashville: Abingdon, 1976.

Peterson, James A. and Barbara Payne. *Love in the Later Years*. New York: Association Press, 1975.

Peterson, James. *Married Love in the Middle Years*. New York: Association Press, 168.

Rogers, Carl. *Becoming Partners: Marriage and Its Alternatives*. New York: Delacorte Press, 1972.

Rogers, Carl. *On Becoming a Person*. Boston: Houghton Mifflin, 1961.

Rutledge, Aaron L. *Premarital Counseling*. Cambridge, Mass.: Schenkman Publishing Co., 1966.

Satir, Virginia. *Peoplemaking*. Palo Alto, Calif.: Science & Behavior Books, 1973.

Schumm, Walter R., and Wallace Denton. "Trends in Premarital Counseling," *The Journal of Marital and Family Therapy*. Volume 5, Number 4, October, 1979.

Sheehy, Gail. *Passages*. New York: E.P. Dutton, 1976.

Smith, Leon. *Family Ministry*. Nashville: Discipleship Resources, 1975.

Smith, Leon, ed. *Homosexuality: In Search of a Christian Understanding*. Nashville: Discipleship Resources, 1981.

Smith, Rebecca M. *Klemer's Marriage and Family Relationships*. New York: Harper & Row, 1975.

Snyder, Ross. *Inscape*. Nashville: Abingdon, 1971.

Stahmann, Robert F., and William J. Hiebert. *Premarital Counseling*. Lexington Mass.: D.C. Heath & Co., 1980.

Stewart, Charles W. *The Minister as Family Counselor*. Nashville: Abingdon, 1979.

Stewart, Charles W. *The Minister as Marriage Counselor*. Nashville: Abingdon, 1970.

Trainer, Joseph B. "Pre-Marital Counseling and Examination." *Journal of Marital and Family Therapy*. April, 1979.

Vincent, Clark. *Human Sexuality in Medical Education and Practice*. Springfield, Ill.: Charles C. Thomas, Publisher, 1968.

Vincent, Clark. *Sexual & Marital Health*. New York: McGraw-Hill, 1973.

Zilbergeld, Bernie. *Male Sexuality*. Boston: Little, Brown, 1978.